*Ninety Days
of Inspirational Readings
to Affirm, Strengthen
and Encourage
the Man Of Character*

BROADMAN
&HOLMAN
PUBLISHERS

© 1998 Broadman & Holman Publishers
All rights reserved
Printed in Belgium
ISBN: 0-8054-9267-4
Dewey Decimal Classification: 242.5
Subject Heading: Bible: Meditations
Library of Congress Catalog Number: 98–5931

Library of Congress Cataloging-in-Publication Data
The one minute Bible : men of character / edited by Lawrence Kimbrough.
    p.   cm.
   ISBN 0-8054-9267-4
   1. Bible—Meditations. 2. Men in the Bible—Meditations. 3. Men—Religious life—Biblical teaching.   I. Kimbrough, Lawrence, 1963–.
BS574.5.054   1998
242'.5—dc21

Table of Contents

- 2. **Noah:** Righteous in His Generation
- 4. **Abraham:** Choosing Peace
- 6. **Abraham:** Interceding for Others
- 8. **Abraham:** Up to the Test
- 10. **Isaac:** A Lifestyle of Prayer
- 12. **Jacob:** Hanging Tough
- 14. **Esau:** Forgiveness without a Trace
- 16. **Joseph:** Staying Sexually Pure
- 18. **Joseph:** Staying Usable
- 20. **Joseph:** Recognizing God's Plan
- 22. **Moses:** Too Scared to Try
- 24. **Moses:** Courageous Leadership
- 26. **Moses:** Open to Advice
- 28. **Moses:** Depending 100 Percent on God
- 30. **Moses:** Interceding for a Nation
- 32. **Aaron:** Caving to the Crowd
- 34. **Bezalel and Oholiab:** Excellence in Their Work
- 36. **Caleb:** Enthusiastic as Ever
- 38. **Phinehas:** Righteous Indignation
- 40. **Joshua:** Filling Big Shoes
- 42. **Gideon:** Fighting Doubts and Fears
- 44. **Jephthah:** Speaking Careless Words
- 46. **Samson:** Dealing with Consequences
- 48. **Boaz:** A Case for Kindness
- 50. **Samuel:** Lifelong Obedience
- 52. **Saul:** A Loser at Leadership
- 54. **Jonathan:** A Friend to the End
- 56. **David:** Bigger Than Betrayal
- 58. **David:** Uninhibited in His Worship
- 60. **David:** Committed to Compassion
- 62. **David:** Ready to Repent
- 64. **David:** Accepting Disappointment
- 66. **David:** Passing Down a Blessing
- 68. **David:** Given to Good Stewardship
- 70. **Solomon:** Choosing Wisdom
- 72. **Solomon:** Turning Away
- 74. **Rehoboam:** In Bad Company
- 76. **Asa:** Confronting Family
- 78. **Ahab:** Recognizing God's Power
- 80. **Elijah:** Dealing with Discouragement
- 82. **Elijah:** Speaking Truth in High Places
- 84. **Jehoshaphat:** Godly Governing
- 86. **Elisha:** Modeling His Mentor
- 88. **Elisha:** Seeing with Spiritual Eyes
- 90. **Uzziah:** Pulled Down by Pride
- 92. **Hezekiah:** Powered by Prayer
- 94. **Josiah:** Renewing the Covenant
- 96. **Ezra:** A Love for God's Word
- 98. **Nehemiah:** Unpolluted by Power

100. **Mordecai:** Advocate for the Oppressed
102. **Haman:** A Prisoner to Prejudice
104. **Job:** Faith That Perseveres
106. **Isaiah:** Fearing God
108. **Jeremiah:** Obedience to His Calling
110. **Shadrach, Meshach, and Abednego:** No Compromise
112. **Daniel:** Faithfulness without Reward
114. **Jonah:** Running from God
116. **Habakkuk:** Trusting God Anyway
118. **Zechariah:** Questioning God
120. **Joseph:** Staying in God's Will
122. **Simeon:** Never Stop Waiting
124. **John the Baptist:** Accepting a Supporting Role
126. **The Centurion:** Submitting to God's Authority
128. **Bartimaeus:** Believing in Miracles
130. **Zacchaeus:** Repaying for His Sins
132. **Nicodemus:** Converted out of His Culture
134. **Thomas:** Seeing Is Believing
136. **Joseph of Arimathea:** Meeting Practical Needs
138. **Peter:** Captured by Conscience
140. **Peter:** Confident in Christ
142. **Peter:** Confronting Indiscretion
144. **Peter:** Overcoming Prejudice
146. **Stephen:** Paying the Ultimate Price
148. **Philip:** Sensitive to the Spirit
150. **Simon the Sorcerer:** Wanting God Selfishly
152. **Ananias:** Believing in Forgiveness
154. **Barnabas:** Encouraging Others
156. **The Philippian Jailer:** Accepting the Gospel
158. **Apollos and Aquila:** Teachers of the Word
160. **Julius:** Kindness in an Unbeliever
162. **Onesimus:** From Useless to Useful
164. **Paul:** Struggling with Sin
166. **Paul:** Love for His People
168. **Paul:** Love for the Church
170. **Paul:** No Lone Ranger
172. **Paul:** Embracing Hardship
174. **Paul:** Humble before God
176. **Paul:** Recognizing His Need for Prayer
178. **John:** Appealing for Love
180. **John:** Open to God's Revelation
183. **Sources**

presented to

_____

by

_____

_____

date

_____

Noah
Righteous in His Generation

from Genesis 6 & 7

Ever think the times couldn't get any worse? Believe it or not, they have been. When God singled out Noah to help keep human history afloat, He was asking him to be obedient in a world where everyone—everyone!—was "evil all the time." Check out Noah's lonely walk.

LOOK AT IT THIS WAY

If you're not careful, you can almost forget that Bible heroes like Noah were real men, living in a real age. But Noah was a real man. And he did live in a real age—building a boat longer than a football field in a land that had never seen rain, preaching God's grace against impending doom for 120 years without a single convert outside his own family, feeling his neighbors' spit in his face for insinuating *they* were the ones who needed help.

A superman would have made it look easy. It took an ordinary man to make it look like God.

First, a Quick Read

The LORD saw how great man's wickedness on the earth had become, and that every inclination of the thoughts of his heart was only evil all the time. . . .

But Noah found favor in the eyes of the LORD.

This is the account of Noah. Noah was a righteous man, blameless among the people of his time, and he walked with God. . . .

Now the earth was corrupt in God's sight and was full of violence. . . . So God said to Noah, "I am going to put an end to all people, for the earth is filled with violence because of them. I am surely going to destroy both them and the earth. So make yourself an ark of cypress wood. . . . I am going to bring floodwaters on the earth to destroy all life under the heavens. . . . But I will establish my covenant with you, and you will enter the ark—you and your sons and your wife and your sons' wives with you." . . .

Noah did everything just as God commanded him.

The LORD then said to Noah, "Go into the ark, you and your whole family, because I have found you righteous in this generation."

Genesis 6:5, 8–9, 11, 13–14a, 17a, 18, 22; 7:1

When You Think about It

These days of darkness are also days of opportunity. But what makes them days of opportunity is the power of light—of good ideas and good people—to pierce and dispel the darkness. Our cultural crisis is at the same time a cultural opportunity.

Jesus said of Himself, "I am the light of the world" (John 8:12). Amazingly, He also said, "You are the light of the world. A city on a hill cannot be hidden" (Matt. 5:14). Of course, our light is totally dependent on His. He is "the true light that gives light to every man" (John 1:9). As Christians concerned about our culture (as all should be), we must ask ourselves, "How can I make the most of the opportunity that is before me to shine as Jesus would? How can I best treat the present crisis as an opportunity, and focus my beam into the present darkness?"

It needs to be said and said continually: The first task of every Christian is to be like Jesus. We are to give ourselves wholly to the pursuit of Christlikeness. We dare not urge in public life what our private lives deny.
—Lawrence F. Burtoft

A good life is a main argument.
—Ben Jonson

> **CHARACTER CHECK**
>
> Ask yourself when you'll finally be ready to forsake everything that keeps you from being faithful to God's calling. If not now, when? Come on! Let's be righteous in our generation.

Abraham
Choosing Peace
from Genesis 13

If anyone had earned the best land, Abraham had. He was the one who had turned his back on everything, pursuing the voice of God no matter the cost. Lot was just along for the ride. But when it became apparent that someone had to give, Abraham took the high moral ground.

Look at It This Way

We fuss at our children for wanting their way, for fighting over who gets to play with the black-haired baby doll or the toy car with the green racing stripes. But some people never outgrow wanting things to go their way, and none of us do without a struggle.

Next time you see a child ruining his whole day over something that seems insignificant, think about the things you lock horns over—a parking space, an undercooked steak, a referee's whistle—and see if a more peaceable response wouldn't look a lot more grown-up.

First, a Quick Read

So Abram went up from Egypt to the Negev, with his wife and everything he had, and Lot went with him. Abram had become very wealthy in livestock and in silver and gold. . . .

Now Lot, who was moving about with Abram, also had flocks and herds and tents. But the land could not support them while they stayed together, for their possessions were so great that they were not able to stay together. And quarreling arose between Abram's herdsmen and the herdsmen of Lot. . . .

So Abram said to Lot, "Let's not have any quarreling between you and me, or between your herdsmen and mine, for we are brothers. Is not the whole land before you? Let's part company. If you go to the left, I'll go to the right; if you go to the right, I'll go to the left."

Lot looked up and saw that the whole plain of the Jordan was well watered, like the garden of the LORD, like the land of Egypt, toward Zoar. (This was before the LORD destroyed Sodom and Gomorrah.)

So Lot chose for himself the whole plain of the Jordan and set out toward the east. The two men parted company.

Genesis 13:1–2, 5–7a, 8–11

When You Think about It

As soon as you begin to live the life of faith in God, fascinating and luxurious prospects will open up before you, and these things are yours by right; but if you are living the life of faith, you will exercise your right to waive your rights and let God choose for you.

God sometimes allows you to get into a place of testing where your own welfare would be the right and proper thing to consider if you were not living a life of faith; but if you are, you will joyfully waive your right and leave God to choose for you.

Whenever *right* is made the guidance in the life, it will blunt the spiritual insight. The great enemy of the life of faith in God is not sin, but the good which is not good enough. The good is always the enemy of the best. It would seem the wisest thing in the world for Abraham to choose; it was his right, and the people around would consider him a fool for not choosing. Many of us do not go on spiritually because we prefer to choose what is right instead of relying on God to choose for us. We have to learn to walk according to the standard which has its eye on God.

—Oswald Chambers

Whenever there is a disposition to quarrel, there you can be certain God does not reign.

—John Calvin

> **CHARACTER CHECK**
>
> When you reach an impasse with someone, choose the way of peace rather than privilege. You'll learn firsthand what Christ meant when He said, "Blessed are the peacemakers" (Matt. 5:9).

Abraham Interceding for Others

from Genesis 18

Lot had done Abraham dirty. And now he was paying for it. The pastures that had looked so green from a distance had hidden dark, ugly corners of sin and perversion. Abraham had good reason to say good riddance. But love and loyalty dropped him to his knees.

Look at It This Way

Abraham's prayer proves two very important things. First, you can feel absolute freedom in God's presence. Prayer is a place where you're welcome, for as long as you like, where you're never an annoyance or bother. It's where God wants you to be.

And second, you can expect an answer from the Lord. Even when your prayers seem to clank against an iron sky and thud untouched at your feet, you can be sure you haven't been dismissed or ignored. Like a clock, God's movements are often undetected, but they're always right on time.

First, a Quick Read

Then the LORD said, "The outcry against Sodom and Gomorrah is so great and their sin so grievous that I will go down and see if what they have done is as bad as the outcry that has reached me. If not, I will know." . . .

Then Abraham approached him and said: "Will you sweep away the righteous with the wicked? What if there are fifty righteous people in the city? Will you really sweep it away and not spare the place for the sake of the fifty righteous people in it? . . .

Then Abraham spoke up again: "Now that I have been so bold as to speak to the Lord, though I am nothing but dust and ashes, what if the number of the righteous is five less than fifty? Will you destroy the whole city because of five people?"

. . . "What if only forty are found there?" . . .

Then he said, "May the Lord not be angry, but let me speak. What if only thirty can be found there?" . . .

Abraham said, "Now that I have been so bold as to speak to the Lord, what if only twenty can be found there?" . . .

Then he said, "May the Lord not be angry, but let me speak just once more. What if only ten can be found there?"

He answered, "For the sake of ten, I will not destroy it."

Genesis 18:20–21, 23–24, 27–28a, 29a, 30a, 31a, 32

When You Think about It

What a mystery of glory there is in prayer! On the one hand, we see God in His holiness and love and power waiting, longing to bless man; and on the other, sinful man on the other end of the scale, bringing down from God by prayer the very life and love of heaven to dwell in his heart.

But how much greater the glory of intercession when a man makes bold to say to God what he desires for others, and seeks to bring down on one soul, or hundreds and thousands, the power of the eternal life with all its blessings.

Intercession! Would one not say that this is the holiest exercise of our boldness as God's children, the highest privilege and enjoyment connected with our communion with God—the power of being used by God as instruments for His great work of making men His habitation and showing forth His glory?

It is when Christians aim at all being bound together to the throne of God, by an unceasing devotion to Jesus Christ, that the church will put on her beautiful garments, and put on her strength, too, and overcome the world.
—Andrew Murray

Nothing makes us love a man so much as praying for him.
—William Law

> **CHARACTER CHECK**
>
> Think of someone who's hurting, who really needs God's help. Carve some time out of your day to plead with God for that person. It'll do more than you know.

Abraham
Up to the Test
from Genesis 22

Just when you think you've got God figured out, just when your future seems to stretch out before you with perfect predictability, that's when God has a way of pressing a new wrinkle into your neat, ironed-out ideas. Like the time He told Abraham that A+B equaled ... WHAT?!?

LOOK AT IT THIS WAY

Abraham's testing foreshadowed the key event on which all Christianity turns—the atoning death of Jesus Christ—when the Lamb of God was provided as the substitute for the sins of the world.

In the same way, God often has more than just you in mind when He allows difficult seasons to move into your life. He also has His eye on your unbelieving coworkers, your doubting relatives, your faltering friends. Your testimony through tough times may be the way God has chosen to speak so that those around you will listen.

First, a Quick Read

Then God said, "Take your son, your only son, Isaac, whom you love, and go to the region of Moriah. Sacrifice him there as a burnt offering...."

Early the next morning Abraham got up and saddled his donkey. He took with him two of his servants and his son Isaac....

Isaac spoke up and said to his father Abraham, "Father?"

"Yes, my son?" Abraham replied.

The fire and wood are here," Isaac said, "but where is the lamb for the burnt offering?"

Abraham answered, "God himself will provide the lamb for the burnt offering, my son." And the two of them went on together.

When they reached the place God had told him about, Abraham built an altar there and arranged the wood on it. He bound his son Isaac and laid him on the altar, on top of the wood. Then he reached out his hand and took the knife to slay his son. But the angel of the LORD called out to him from heaven, "Abraham! Abraham!"

"Here I am," he replied.

"Do not lay a hand on the boy," he said. "Do not do anything to him. Now I know that you fear God, because you have not withheld from me your son, your only son."

Genesis 22:2a, 3a, 7

When You Think about It

Abraham loved God. But he also loved Isaac, the child of promise. This young lad had become the center of his life. Perhaps at this moment in his experience, if he were asked whom he loved more—Isaac or God—it may have been difficult for him to answer.

Get the picture? God tested Abraham in the most emotionally sensitive area of his life. Was he willing to put his Lord before Isaac? Was he willing to obey God rather than following his own desires?

You, of course, know what happened. Abraham passed the test. His love for God was stronger than his love for Isaac. He demonstrated this love through unwavering trust and confidence in his heavenly Father.

Today God often tests us in these sensitive areas of our lives. What is most important to us? Where does our security lie? We mustn't be surprised if we're suddenly confronted with a choice between our dearest possessions and the God we also love. It's in moments like these that we begin to understand how deep our love for God really is—or isn't.

—Gene A. Getz

Satan tempts us that he may bring out all the evil that is in our hearts; God tries or tests us that He may bring out all the good.

—F. B. Meyer

> **CHARACTER CHECK**
>
> Submitting to God's testing, even if it's something you've sort of brought on yourself, is always the shortest way to reclaiming your peace, steadying your course, becoming more like Christ.

Isaac
A Lifestyle of Prayer

from Genesis 24 & 25; James 5

There's not a lot said about Isaac in the Bible. He's remembered more for being a child on his way to the chopping block and an old man conned by his conniving son. But look closer and you'll see another side of Isaac's character—a man in the habit of communing with God.

First, a Quick Read

Now Isaac had come from Beer Lahai Roi, for he was living in the Negev. He went out to the field one evening to meditate, and as he looked up, he saw camels approaching. Rebekah also looked up and saw Isaac. She got down from her camel and asked the servant, "Who is that man in the field coming to meet us?" "He is my master," the servant answered. So she took her veil and covered herself.

Then the servant told Isaac all he had done. Isaac brought her into the tent of his mother Sarah, and he married Rebekah. So she became his wife, and he loved her; and Isaac was comforted after his mother's death....

... Isaac was forty years old when he married Rebekah daughter of Bethuel the Aramean from Paddan Aram and sister of Laban the Aramean.

Isaac prayed to the LORD on behalf of his wife, because she was barren. The LORD answered his prayer, and his wife Rebekah became pregnant.

Genesis 24:62–67; 25:20–21

If you remain in me and my words remain in you, ask whatever you wish, and it will be given you. *John 15:7*

The prayer of a righteous man is powerful and effective.

James 5:16b

LOOK AT IT THIS WAY

Someone once said to be careful who you're talking to when you're by yourself—in the car, behind the lawnmower, through the wakeful hours of the night. Lots of people spend those dead-air times trying to solve their work problems, or worrying about how to pay for a new transmission, or winning imaginary arguments with their spouse.

Wouldn't that time be a lot better spent praying to your Father for help, getting His wise advice on the matter, and letting Him sweat the details?

When You Think about It

Several years ago, while Jimmy Carter campaigned for the presidency of the United States, he became the butt of innumerable jokes about his spiritual life. Responding to a reporter's question about his prayer life, candidate Carter explained that he prayed all the time. He spoke of praying while waiting for a traffic light to change, while walking, and during all kinds of other engagements. Many members of the media judged Carter's comments to be hilarious, if not ridiculous. Scores of people read his comments about prayer and laughed. But Jimmy Carter's revelation about his personal prayer life provided an excellent insight into the meaning of God's expectation of all of us—that we pray persistently.

A lot of people declare that they pray when they feel like it or really want to. At other times, they don't bother themselves about the need to pray. We can no more discard praying because we are not in the mood than we can stop breathing because we don't feel like making the effort. Regular communication with God is a basic necessity in the lives of all who love God.
—C. Welton Gaddy

Fellowship with God as an activity will issue in fellowship with God as an attitude.
—G. Campbell Morgan

> **CHARACTER CHECK**
>
> Make your first conscious thought of the day a word of praise to God and commit yourself to prayer every time the thought of God enters your mind all day long. Never resist the impulse to pray.

Jacob
Hanging Tough

from Genesis 32

Life wasn't easy for Jacob. Confused by his mother, threatened by his brother, tricked by his father-in-law, he had learned his lessons the hard way. But what he often lacked in sterling character, he made up for with dogged determination. And God found a way to use it for good.

Look at It This Way

God's choice of the name Israel for this patriarch of His chosen people (meaning "he strives against God") could not have been more prophetic. The history of His chosen people has been one of struggle and strife. Yet even though they were taken captive into Egypt, into Babylon and Assyria, dispersed to the ends of the earth and despised by those still intent on pushing them into the sea, they have remained. Why? Because of God's covenant and His ability to keep His promises. Indeed, the only thing stronger than Israel's will has been the God who stubbornly preserves them through time.

First, a Quick Read

That night Jacob got up and took his two wives, his two maidservants and his eleven sons and crossed the ford of the Jabbok. After he had sent them across the stream, he sent over all his possessions. So Jacob was left alone, and a man wrestled with him till daybreak. When the man saw that he could not overpower him, he touched the socket of Jacob's hip so that his hip was wrenched as he wrestled with the man. Then the man said, "Let me go, for it is daybreak."

But Jacob replied, "I will not let you go unless you bless me."

The man asked him, "What is your name?"

"Jacob," he answered.

Then the man said, "Your name will no longer be Jacob, but Israel, because you have struggled with God and with men and have overcome."

Jacob said, "Please tell me your name."

But he replied, "Why do you ask my name?" Then he blessed him there.

So Jacob called the place Peniel, saying, "It is because I saw God face to face, and yet my life was spared."

Genesis 32:22–30

When You Think about It

Throughout his life, Jacob had gotten away with trickery so often, it was his standard operating procedure. But now the Lord said, "I'm going to see how badly he wants to live for Me. How badly does he really want My blessing and to fulfill My purpose?" He had to wrestle for his destiny with the Almighty and grab hold of his calling.

Wrestling with God will dislocate self-made plans, dreams, and desires and expose you to the Supreme Power. The mark of a real man of God is the one who walks with a spiritual limp. It proves he has been in the battle. Many Christians love to share their testimonies about great triumphs, but the Lord gets more glory when you share your struggles.

If you want to answer God's call on your life, then you must pursue it with the same unyielding effort that drove Jacob to wrestle all night with the Almighty. You must desperately want the covenant that God promises to those who cling to Him. Maturity doesn't come with age but with striving to know the Lord, submission to the level of knowledge He has revealed to you, and acceptance of responsibility.
—Tom Sirotnak

There are no victories at bargain prices.
—Dwight D. Eisenhower

> **CHARACTER CHECK**
>
> Has God given you a dream? A picture of what He wants you to do? To be? Then hang in there. Embrace your calling. If it's from Him, He'll bring it to pass.

Esau
Forgiveness without a Trace

from Genesis 27; 32;33

Jacob had cheated his brother Esau out of all that ever mattered to him: his father's blessing, his confirmation of wealth, lands, and honor. Now Jacob was going to pay with his life. But somehow God wormed a sliver of love under the tough, hairy hide of this rugged outdoorsman.

LOOK AT IT THIS WAY

Jesus said that an unforgiving spirit hinders the ability to receive forgiveness from God. But—like many things in His kingdom—getting there requires traveling backward from human thinking. You don't focus on your own shortcomings, trying to reform them through mind games and willpower. You focus on God's forgiveness of you, His love for you, His willingness to extend the freedom of righteousness to you. This is always the way. You fix the problem by fixing your eyes, your attention, your concentration on Jesus—and letting Him fix you the right way.

First, a Quick Read

Esau held a grudge against Jacob because of the blessing his father had given him. He said to himself, "The days of mourning for my father are near; then I will kill my brother Jacob." . . .

Jacob sent messengers ahead of him to his brother Esau in the land of Seir, the country of Edom. He instructed them: "This is what you are to say to my master Esau: 'Your servant Jacob says, I have been staying with Laban and have remained there till now. I have cattle and donkeys, sheep and goats, menservants and maidservants. Now I am sending this message to my lord, that I may find favor in your eyes.'" . . .

Jacob looked up and there was Esau, coming with his four hundred men. . . ." He himself went on ahead and bowed down to the ground seven times as he approached his brother.

But Esau ran to meet Jacob and embraced him; he threw his arms around his neck and kissed him. And they wept. . . .

"No, please!" said Jacob. "If I have found favor in your eyes, accept this gift from me. For to see your face is like seeing the face of God, now that you have received me favorably.

Genesis 27:41; 32:3–5; 33:1a, 3–4, 10

When You Think about It

Leonardo da Vinci had a violent quarrel with a fellow painter shortly before he began work on *The Last Supper*. As he began to paint, his anger led him to paint the face of the man who was now his enemy into the face of Judas. This was da Vinci's revenge, and he was gleeful over what he had done. But when he started to paint the face of Christ, his best efforts failed. He could no longer see the Savior he longed to honor. Through his struggle, he realized that he must forgive his fellow painter and erase his face from that of Judas. Only then was da Vinci able to see Jesus clearly and paint His face onto the canvas of *The Last Supper*.

Like daVinci, we too have difficulty seeing Jesus clearly when the sin of unforgiveness comes between us and someone who has offended us. Forgiveness must be complete. It must come from the heart. We must put all thought of the wrongdoing from us and begin anew. That's what God does for us. That's what we must do for others.

—Chip Ricks

Let there be no brother who has sinned, no matter how seriously, who would look into your eyes seeking forgiveness, and go away without it.

—Francis of Assisi

CHARACTER CHECK

Has Esau's story brought someone to your mind? That person you said you could never forgive? Bring this situation to God today. He knows what it takes to do it.

JOSEPH
Staying Sexually Pure

from Genesis 39

His master's wife wasn't just casually flirting with Joseph. She was coming on to him big-time, flaunting the kind of half-dressed half-truths that any man with half a hormone would have a tough time resisting. But the way he played it was a pure stroke of integrity.

First, a Quick Read

Now Joseph was well-built and handsome, and after a while his master's wife took notice of Joseph and said, "Come to bed with me!"

But he refused. "With me in charge," he told her, "my master does not concern himself with anything in the house; everything he owns he has entrusted to my care.... My master has withheld nothing from me except you, because you are his wife. How then could I do such a wicked thing and sin against God?" And though she spoke to Joseph day after day, he refused to go to bed with her or even be with her.

One day he went into the house to attend to his duties, and none of the household servants was inside. She caught him by his cloak and said, "Come to bed with me!" But he left his cloak in her hand and ran out of the house....

She kept his cloak beside her until his master came home. Then she told him this story: "That Hebrew slave you brought us came to me to make sport of me. But as soon as I screamed for help, he left his cloak beside me and ran out of the house."...

Joseph's master took him and put him in prison.

Genesis 39:6b–8, 9b–12, 16–18, 20a

LOOK AT IT THIS WAY

Placing your life under the lordship of Jesus Christ doesn't mean turning your back on pleasure. It means discovering "eternal pleasures" from the hand of God (Ps. 16:11). All that the world's pleasures can offer is slick advertising. Underneath the smile and the swimsuit is pain, loneliness, heartbreak, emptiness, and the sickening, sour taste of detesting yourself and the unreliable piece of weakness you really are.

That's a strange way to define pleasure, but it's the best the world's pleasures have to offer. Your temptation to want them is really your hunger for more of "the splendor of holiness" (Ps. 96:9).

When You Think about It

It's hard to miss God's concern for purity. He demanded the use of pure gold in the construction of the tabernacle; He prescribed pure incense for use in worship; He required pure animals for sacrifice; He commanded pure hearts, pure religion, and pure relationships.

In other words, the Model Father communicates—in contrast to modern culture, peer pressure, and media messages—that *purity is good*. The Model Father commands purity because purity is something He values. And purity is something He values because He Himself is pure.

That's the kind of father I want to be. I want my kids to know that *purity is good*. I want my children to understand that purity is not something to be ashamed of or embarrassed about. I want them to reject the fascination with immorality and deviancy that their culture, peers, and the media so often display. I want them to know that I value purity, like the Father I serve and seek to emulate. I want them to see the benefits of purity. And I want them to see a godly standard of sexual purity *in me*.
—Josh McDowell

Purity demands that we know ahead of time what we will do when temptation comes.
—T. W. Hunt

CHARACTER CHECK

Usually, the knowledge that someone is watching is enough to squash sexual temptation. Make it your daily, ongoing habit to "set the LORD always before" you (Ps. 16:8).

JOSEPH
Staying Usable

from Genesis 41

If Joseph ever shook his fist into the Egyptian sky and cursed the God whose covenant required so much from him, you never hear of it. Surely there were moments of sorrowful surrender. But he never quit on God. And God never quit finding ways to use Joseph for His glory.

LOOK AT IT THIS WAY

It doesn't always seem like it—God graciously hides it from you and does his work behind the scenes—but you're never really in control of your circumstances. One violent thunderstorm, one slick sheet of ice, one fuzzy spot on an x-ray, and your whole concept of normal can change in a heartbeat.

But circumstances are not your boss. They may add new boundaries to the playing field or throw a short-term advantage to the enemy, but God has a winning strategy for every situation.

First, a Quick Read

Then Joseph said to Pharaoh, . . . "Seven years of great abundance are coming throughout the land of Egypt, but seven years of famine will follow them. . . .

"Let Pharaoh appoint commissioners over the land to take a fifth of the harvest of Egypt during the seven years of abundance. They should collect all the food of these good years that are coming and store up the grain under the authority of Pharaoh, to be kept in the cities for food. This food should be held in reserve for the country, to be used during the seven years of famine that will come upon Egypt."

The plan seemed good to Pharaoh and to all his officials. So Pharaoh asked them, "Can we find anyone like this man, one in whom is the spirit of God?"

Then Pharaoh said to Joseph, "Since God has made all this known to you, there is no one so discerning and wise as you. You shall be in charge of my palace, and all my people are to submit to your orders. Only with respect to the throne will I be greater than you." . . .

. . . And Joseph went out from Pharaoh's presence and traveled throughout Egypt.

Genesis 41:25a, 29–30a, 34–36a, 37–40, 46b

When You Think about It

We get in trouble when we try to get God to tell us if He wants us to be a Christian business person, a music director, an education director, a preacher, or a missionary. God doesn't usually give you a one-time assignment and leave you there forever. Yes, you may be placed in one job at one place for a long time; but God's assignments come to you on a daily basis.

He calls you to a relationship where He is Lord—where you are willing to do and be anything He chooses. If you will respond to Him as Lord, He may lead you to do and be things you would have never dreamed of. If you don't follow Him as Lord, you may lock yourself into a job or an assignment and miss something God wants to do through you.

Your response should be something like this: "Lord, I will do anything that your kingdom requires of me. Wherever You want me to be, I'll go. Whatever the circumstances, I'm willing to follow. If you want to meet a need through my life, I am your servant; and I will do whatever is required."

—Henry Blackaby

Do not pray for tasks equal to your powers. Pray for powers equal to your tasks.

—Keith Brooks

CHARACTER CHECK

Does God have you where He wants you? Does He know that with one spiritual signal He can move you into the place that's right for Him and best for you?

Joseph
Recognizing God's Plan

from Genesis 45

Whether it happened all at once or gradually came into view, Joseph finally saw what God was up to in his life. So, *of course* it took a wicked plot by his brothers. *Of course,* it took extra prison time. *Of course,* it took a famine. Only God could have put all that together.

LOOK AT IT THIS WAY

"God loves you and offers a wonderful plan for your life." It's the first of the *Four Spiritual Laws.* And it reveals a fundamental need in every person—to realize that God has made plans for you, "plans to prosper you and not to harm you, plans to give you hope and a future" (Jer. 29:11).

Knowing what those plans are isn't always easy. God's reasons are rarely on the surface. But would you want them if they were? Would you believe in the power of God if He couldn't perform His will through the most unbelievable of ways?

First, a Quick Read

Then Joseph could no longer control himself before all his attendants, and he cried out, "Have everyone leave my presence!" So there was no one with Joseph when he made himself known to his brothers. And he wept so loudly that the Egyptians heard him, and Pharaoh's household heard about it.

Joseph said to his brothers, "I am Joseph! Is my father still living?" But his brothers were not able to answer him, because they were terrified at his presence.

Then Joseph said to his brothers, "Come close to me." When they had done so, he said, "I am your brother Joseph, the one you sold into Egypt! And now, do not be distressed and do not be angry with yourselves for selling me here, because it was to save lives that God sent me ahead of you. For two years now there has been famine in the land, and for the next five years there will not be plowing and reaping. But God sent me ahead of you to preserve for you a remnant on earth and to save your lives by a great deliverance."

Genesis 45:1–7

When You Think about It

Blind faith is not a biblical concept. It's not that we believe in spite of the fact that we're in an unending night; rather, we believe because we *see* the invisible light and are "certain of what we do not see" with our human eyes.

We trust in Someone who defines the word *reliable*. We can know from God's Word the kind of trials that we might face, and we can know from God's Word that He will deliver us. We can understand what God means and expects, and we can discern whether or not we're in line with those expectations. In fact, we *must* discern this, or we'll never know whether we're on the right path—whether we should persist in what we're doing or whether we should stop.

The Christian's call is not to blind, confused floundering, hanging on to God even though we can't know Him or understand Him. The call is to know our great God and Father, to understand His intentions, and—by His grace, wisdom, and strength—to walk in good ways. To know Him is to love Him—and to understand that He's the God of love, not luck.

—James R. Lucas

To live is to suffer; to survive is to find meaning in suffering.

—Viktor Frankl

> **CHARACTER CHECK**
>
> Trying to think the way God thinks requires getting to know Him better, learning how to be ever aware of His presence. You're doing it right now. Stick with Him.

Moses Too Scared to Try

from Exodus 3 & 4

Moses had buried his zeal and confidence long ago in the blistering sands of Midian, far from the princely pomp of Egypt. When he looked in the mirror now, all he saw was an eighty-year-old waste of time . . . and . . . wait a minute . . . some kind of bush on fire or something.

First, a Quick Read

The Lord said, "I have indeed seen the misery of my people in Egypt. . . . So now, go. I am sending you to Pharaoh to bring my people the Israelites out of Egypt."

But Moses said to God, "Who am I, that I should go to Pharaoh and bring the Israelites out of Egypt?

And God said, "I will be with you.". . .

Moses said to God, "Suppose I go to the Israelites and say to them, 'The God of your fathers has sent me to you,' and they ask me, 'What is his name?' Then what shall I tell them?" . . .

. . . "What if they do not believe me or listen to me and say, 'The Lord did not appear to you'?" . . .

. . . "O Lord, I have never been eloquent, neither in the past nor since you have spoken to your servant. I am slow of speech and tongue."

The Lord said to him, "Who gave man his mouth? Who makes him deaf or mute? Who gives him sight or makes him blind? Is it not I, the Lord? Now go; I will help you speak and will teach you what to say."

But Moses said, "O Lord, please send someone else to do it."

Exodus 3:7a, 10–12a, 13, 4:1, 10–13

Look at It This Way

Settledness is the enemy of service. When you get comfortable spending your nights watching television documentaries or ingesting more news than you could use in two lifetimes, then God's gentle nudging for you to—let's say, call someone on your church's prayer list—is easy to shoot down. You fear those awkward pauses in conversation. You worry you might catch someone at a bad time. You might not know them well enough and come off sounding nosy. Fear comes in all kinds of excuses—and leaves you settling for much less than God's best.

When You Think about It

Want to know the shortest route to ineffectiveness? Start running scared. Try to cover every base at all times. Become paranoid over your front, your flanks, and your rear. Think about every possible peril, focus on the dangers, concern yourself with the "what ifs' instead of the "why nots?" Take no chances. Say no to courage and yes to caution. Expect the worst. Play your cards close to the vest. Let fear run wild. "To him who is in fear," said Sophocles, "everything rustles."

How much better to take on a few ornery bears and lions, as David did. They ready us for giants like Goliath. How much more thrilling to step out into the Red Sea like Moses and watch God part the waters. Sure makes for exciting stuff to talk about while trudging around a miserable wilderness for the next forty years. How much more interesting to set sail for Jerusalem, like Paul, "not knowing what will happen to me there," than to spend one's days in monotonous Miletus, listening for footsteps and watching dull sunsets. Guard your heart from overprotection!
—Charles Swindoll

We are all faced with great opportunities, brilliantly disguised as impossible situations.
—Truett Cathy

CHARACTER CHECK

Is there something you know God expects of you, but you're afraid you'll mess it up or look foolish? Put fear in its place. Let God decide what you can handle.

Moses
Courageous Leadership

from Exodus 14

You've seen the movie. Wave after wave of Israelites, joyfully taking their first free steps outside Egyptian bondage. But hardly were they out of town before the dancing turned to daggers—all pointed at Moses. The old coward in him had a chance to run. Instead, he took a stand.

LOOK AT IT THIS WAY

One of the most challenging frustrations of leadership is realizing that those who follow don't often see things the way you do. With the Egyptian hordes thundering on one side and the waves lapping the shore on the other, the Israelites saw a dead end. But Moses saw two protective walls of water and a clear path to God's deliverance.

When others don't share your enthusiasm or your willingness to sacrifice for an unseen, uncertain goal, do what Moses did. Communicate your vision with clarity and conviction. And trust the Lord to bring His results to pass.

First, a Quick Read

When the king of Egypt was told that the people had fled, Pharaoh and his officials changed their minds about them and said, "What have we done? We have let the Israelites go and have lost their services!" So he had his chariot made ready and took his army with him.

As Pharaoh approached, the Israelites looked up, and there were the Egyptians, marching after them. They were terrified and cried out to the LORD. They said to Moses, "Was it because there were no graves in Egypt that you brought us to the desert to die? What have you done to us by bringing us out of Egypt? Didn't we say to you in Egypt, 'Leave us alone; let us serve the Egyptians'? It would have been better for us to serve the Egyptians than to die in the desert!"

Moses answered the people, "Do not be afraid. Stand firm and you will see the deliverance the LORD will bring you today. The Egyptians you see today you will never see again. The LORD will fight for you; you need only to be still."

Then Moses stretched out his hand over the sea, and all that night the LORD drove the sea back with a strong east wind and turned it into dry land.

Exodus 14:5–6, 10–14, 21a

When You Think about It

You cannot retreat; you cannot go forward; you are shut up on the right hand and on the left; what are you going to do now? The Master's words to you are, "Stand firm."

Despair whispers, "Lie down and die; give it all up." But God would have us put on a cheerful courage, and even in our worst times, rejoice in His love and faithfulness. *Cowardice* says, "Retreat; go back to the worldling's way of action; you cannot play the Christian's part, it is too difficult. Relinquish your principles." *Precipitancy* cries, "Do something. Stir yourself; to stand still and wait is sheer idleness." *Presumption* boasts, "If the sea is before you, march into it and expect a miracle."

But *Faith* listens neither to Presumption, nor to Despair, nor to Cowardice, nor to Precipitancy, but it hears God say, "Stand firm," and immovable as a rock it stands. "*Stand* firm—keep the posture of an upright person, ready for action, expecting further orders, cheerfully and patiently awaiting the directing voice; and it will not be long before God shall say to you, as distinctly as Moses said it to the people of Israel, "Go forward."

—Charles Spurgeon

He feared man so little because he feared God so much.
—A tombstone epitaph in St. Paul's Cathedral, London

CHARACTER CHECK

Courage wouldn't be courageous if it always came easily. Be willing to stand alone even when everyone else has given up. That's the defining mark of a leader.

Moses
Open to Advice
from Exodus 18

His father-in-law was coming to town. And even though Moses had stared down a stubborn Pharaoh and assumed leadership for an entire nation since he and Jethro last had seen each other, Jethro still saw room for improvement. And Moses saw wisdom worth listening to.

First, a Quick Read

Jethro, Moses' father-in-law, together with Moses' sons and wife, came to him in the desert, where he was camped near the mountain of God. . . .

When his father-in-law saw all that Moses was doing for the people, he said, "What is this you are doing for the people? Why do you alone sit as judge, while all these people stand around you from morning till evening?"

Moses answered him, "Because the people come to me to seek God's will." . . .

Moses' father-in-law replied, "What you are doing is not good. You and these people who come to you will only wear yourselves out. The work is too heavy for you; you cannot handle it alone. Listen now to me and I will give you some advice. . . . If you do this and God so commands, you will be able to stand the strain, and all these people will go home satisfied."

Moses listened to his father-in-law and did everything he said. He chose capable men from all Israel and made them leaders of the people. . . . The difficult cases they brought to Moses, but the simple ones they decided themselves.

Exodus 18:5, 14–15, 17–19a, 23–25a, 26b

LOOK AT IT THIS WAY

The Bible makes it clear that Moses had great respect for his father-in-law. So even though Moses didn't exactly ask for it, he seemed genuinely happy to get Jethro's take on the situation.

But sometimes, words of advice come from people you *don't* respect, *don't* like, whose opinions are about as welcome as a first-of-the-month plumbing repair—if they're even *that* reasonable. But your character shows through when you can see past the messenger and spot the hidden value in the message. Hard lessons can often be the best ones.

When You Think about It

Former UCLA basketball coach John Wooden is an inspiring model of personal growth. He continually developed himself, and he did the same with his players, trying to help them reach their potential. Wooden recognized that the greatest obstacle to growth isn't ignorance: It's knowledge. The more you learn, the greater the chance you'll think you know it all. And if that happens, you become unteachable, and you are no longer growing—or improving.

Wooden kept learning and growing, even while he was at the top of his profession. For instance, after he had already won a national championship, an accomplishment that most college coaches never achieve, he scrapped the offense he had used for years and learned a completely new one in order to maximize the potential of his new team and the talents of one player: Lewis Alcindor, now known as Kareem Abdul-Jabbar. The result was that he and his teams moved to an even higher level of play and won three consecutive national championships. And if you are to reach your potential, you have to keep growing just as John Wooden did. When you remain teachable, your potential is almost limitless.

—John Maxwell

It's what you learn after you know it all that counts.

—John Wooden

> **CHARACTER CHECK**
>
> No matter where you are, no matter what you've achieved, no matter how much you know, there's always someone you can learn from. Never get too big for a little advice.

Moses
Depending 100 Percent on God

from Exodus 33

Moses had done a lot of marvelous things as the leader of the Hebrews. Many unbelievable miracles had occurred at the raising of his staff. But as strong and respected a leader as Moses had become, nothing scared him more than making a move without God.

LOOK AT IT THIS WAY

Running ahead of God is a dangerous game. It's like the sudden rush of fear and exposure a deer must feel when it wanders into a misty morning clearing and hears the leathery stretch of a bow string. What seemed normal and safe now smells of imminent danger. No longer can the deer trust the thick density of trees and underbrush for protection. It's on its own now. Good luck.

It doesn't take a genius to figure out that running ahead of God can become a dead sprint into trouble.

First, a Quick Read

Then the LORD said to Moses, "Leave this place, you and the people you brought up out of Egypt, and go up to the land I promised on oath to Abraham, Isaac and Jacob. But I will not go with you, because you are a stiff-necked people and I might destroy you on the way." . . .

Moses said to the LORD, "You have been telling me, . . . 'Lead these people,' but you have not let me know whom you will send with me. If you are pleased with me, teach me your ways so I may know you and continue to find favor with you. Remember that this nation is your people."

The LORD replied, "My Presence will go with you, and I will give you rest."

Then Moses said to him, "If your Presence does not go with us, do not send us up from here. How will anyone know that you are pleased with me and with your people unless you go with us? What else will distinguish me and your people from all the other people on the face of the earth?"

And the LORD said to Moses, "I will do the very thing you have asked, because I am pleased with you and I know you by name."

Exodus 33:1a, 3b, 12a, 13–17

When You Think about It

The people who do God's work God's way don't wait until their efforts fail before they begin trusting Him. They *begin* their projects as dependent people. And in most cases, they maintain their dependent spirit to the end. On occasion when they do begin trusting in their own strength, God always lets them fall flat on their faces.

God will use various people and resources to provide for us. But HE is the source. Remembering that is the key to staying dependent. We have a tendency to confuse the gift with the giver. It is easy to get our eyes focused on the provision rather than the provider. When that happens, our loyalty and trust shift as well. We begin seeking things and people rather than God. Without realizing it, we become idolaters.

God is the source of everything you need. Your children, job, spouse, and friends are only tools He uses to meet the needs in your life. He, however, is the source. Any or all of these things could disappear tomorrow. But your needs will not go unmet. For nothing can separate you from the Source.
—Charles Stanley

Nothing is too great and nothing is too small to commit into the hands of the Lord.
—A. W. Pink

> **CHARACTER CHECK**
>
> Total and complete dependence on God will require a fair amount of waiting. Ask God for the wisdom to discern the times when waiting is your best course of action.

Moses Interceding for a Nation

from Numbers 14

God's words in the following passages are hard to understand. But one thing comes through loud and clear. He's serious about sin and the stain it leaves on His name. No one knew this holy side of God better than Moses did—or had more faith in His patience, love, and forgiveness.

Look at It This Way

It's easy to look back on the failures of the Hebrew people and roll our eyes in judgmental disbelief. Compared to them, we look pretty good. But first, realize that we're reading selected events that span hundreds of years from Moses to the judges to David and beyond. Their forgetfulness of God's miraculous provision was not always as overnight as it appears. And second, let's ask ourselves how our own spiritual history would appear if it were published in an honest manner, slanted to the side of God's holiness. Yes, we need to pray.

First, a Quick Read

The LORD said to Moses, "How long will these people treat me with contempt? How long will they refuse to believe in me, in spite of all the miraculous signs I have performed among them? I will strike them down with a plague and destroy them, but I will make you into a nation greater and stronger than they."

Moses said to the LORD, "Then the Egyptians will hear about it! . . . And they will tell the inhabitants of this land about it. They have already heard that you, O LORD, are with these people and that you, O LORD, have been seen face to face, that your cloud stays over them, and that you go before them in a pillar of cloud by day and a pillar of fire by night. If you put these people to death all at one time, the nations who have heard this report about you will say, 'The LORD was not able to bring these people into the land he promised them on oath; so he slaughtered them in the desert.'

". . . In accordance with your great love, forgive the sin of these people, just as you have pardoned them from the time they left Egypt until now."

The LORD replied, "I have forgiven them, as you asked."

Numbers 14:11–13a, 14–16, 19–20

When You Think about It

For the Christian, prayer must play the central role in any program of social reform. The Scriptures tell us that apart from Christ, we accomplish nothing of lasting value.

Our desire to see society restored in justice and truth inevitably comes down to the individual men and women who make up society. The battle in which we are engaged is for hearts and minds. We certainly have our part to play, and play it we must. But in the final analysis, only the Spirit of God can change the soul of man.

A change of heart on a scale large enough to change the direction of society is what is meant by revival and reformation. Such events simply cannot be engineered, though they may be sought after with great passion. Nearly every great movement of social reform has come as a result of spiritual revival, and nearly every revival was born of prayer.

Regardless of whatever else we may believe about the church's responsibility regarding social action, surely we can agree that prayer for our communities, government, and leaders is a mandate for the Christian personally and the church collectively.

—John Eldredge

I have been driven many times upon my knees by the overwhelming conviction that I had nowhere else to go.

—Abraham Lincoln

> **CHARACTER CHECK**
>
> Setting aside certain days of the week to pray for particular people and concerns gives your prayer life a well-rounded framework. Choose one day to intercede for the nations.

Aaron Caving to the Crowd

from Exodus 32

It had been weeks since Moses was last seen, disappearing into the thick, thundering smoke of Sinai. People were starting to talk. Deep down Aaron knew there was no need to panic. Surely God's promises were trustworthy. But hey, these poll numbers don't lie.

Look at It This Way

Think back to the scene at the burning bush. None of God's visual aids were working on Moses—not seeing his staff double as a snake, not watching his hand turn white with leprosy. Nothing—until God got mad and told him he could take along his big brother, Aaron. *Oh, well, fine. Why didn't you say so?*

Funny how our perceptions of people can be so drastically different from God's. To Moses, Aaron was IT. Big, strong, savvy. But God knew who was really the stronger of the two.

First, a Quick Read

When the People saw that Moses was so long in coming down from the mountain, they gathered around Aaron and said, "Come, make us gods who will go before us. As for this fellow Moses who brought us up out of Egypt, we don't know what has happened to him."

Aaron answered them, "Take off the gold earrings that your wives, your sons and your daughters are wearing, and bring them to me."

He took what they handed him and made it into an idol cast in the shape of a calf, fashioning it with a tool. . . .

When Moses approached the camp and saw the calf and the dancing, his anger burned and he threw the tablets out of his hands, breaking them to pieces at the foot of the mountain. . . .

He said to Aaron, "What did these people do to you, that you led them into such great sin?"

"Do not be angry, my lord," Aaron answered. "You know how prone these people are to evil. They said to me, 'Make us gods who will go before us.' . . . So I told them, 'Whoever has any gold jewelry, take it off.' Then they gave me the gold, and I threw it into the fire, and out came this calf!"

Exodus 32:1–2, 4a, 19, 21–23a, 24

When You Think about It

Some charitably suppose that when Aaron told them to break off their earrings and bring them to him, he did it with design to crush the proposal, believing that though their covetousness would have them lavish gold out of the bag to make an idol of, yet their pride would not have suffered them to part with their golden earrings.

Some think that Aaron chose this figure for a sign or token of the divine presence, because he thought the head and horns of an ox a proper emblem of the divine power, and yet, being so plain and common a thing, he hoped the people would not be so sottish as to worship it.

The Jews have a tradition that his colleague, Hur, opposed it and the people fell upon him and stoned him (and therefore we never read of him after) and that this frightened Aaron into compliance.

And God left him to himself to teach us what the best of men are when they are so left, that we may cease from man, that he who thinks he stands may take heed lest he fall.
—Matthew Henry

We ask what men will think; what others will say. A man has gotten some way in the Christian life when he has learned to say, humbly yet majestically, "I dare to be alone."
—Forbes W. Robertson

Character Check

Who's the crowd you have the hardest time standing up to? Folks at work? Your friends? Your family? The only audience you need to worry about pleasing is God.

Bezalel and Oholiab
Excellence in Their Work

from Exodus 35; 36; 39

Not all the men of character in the Bible are household names. Hidden quietly on the back side of the Book of Exodus, far from the high-speed chases and political intrigue of the first half, lie two men who get special note for simply doing their job. And doing it well.

Look at It This Way

One look at the landscape of today's workplace, and the view is frightening. Maybe it's just our rosy-colored feelings for a bygone era. But maybe not. Quality and service aren't always easy to find.

But look on the bright side. The market for excellence is more open than ever. If you are willing to model the principles of Scripture—out serving, putting others first, going the second mile—you'll stand head and shoulders above the crowd. And even better than that, your witness for Christ will stand the test of your actions.

First, a Quick Read

Then Moses said to the Israelites, "See, the LORD has chosen Bezalel son of Uri, the son of Hur, of the tribe of Judah, and he has filled him with the Spirit of God, with skill, ability and knowledge in all kinds of crafts—to make artistic designs for work in gold, silver and bronze, to cut and set stones, to work in wood and to engage in all kinds of artistic craftsmanship. And he has given both him and Oholiab son of Ahisamach, of the tribe of Dan, the ability to teach others. He has filled them with skill to do all kinds of work as craftsmen, designers, embroiderers in blue, purple and scarlet yarn and fine linen, and weavers—all of them master craftsmen and designers. So Bezalel, Oholiab and every skilled person to whom the LORD has given skill and ability to know how to carry out all the work of constructing the sanctuary are to do the work just as the LORD has commanded."

Moses inspected the work and saw that they had done it just as the LORD had commanded. So Moses blessed them.

Exodus 35:30–36:1; 39:43

When You Think about It

The second commandment rang like a death knell in the heart and head of Bezalel: No graven images. He had learned his craft in Egypt, the most advanced civilization of the world. He dreamed of the day when he would create statuary that would last the ages. But now, while his fellow artists back in Egypt were pressing forward to perfection, he must stay behind.

It's over. Something in him dies. He feels almost an irresistible temptation to rebel. But then, Moses says, "Bezalel, once more—only once more—you are to work. I want you to make the masterpiece of your life—two cherubim for the ark, the last statuary figures an Israelite will ever make. But don't expect human eyes to ever look upon them. They will be placed in the holy of holies, where no human eyes will ever see them, hidden in a dark room with God for all time."

Are you willing to give your best when nobody knows about it at all? Are you willing to leave your work in the holy place of God, and let God and God alone know what you've done?
—L. H. Hardwick, Jr.

Life's greatest joys are not what one does apart from the work of one's life, but *with* the work of one's life.
—William J. Bennett

> **CHARACTER CHECK**
>
> If you have children at home, make it a priority to model and instill excellence into them—a willing, unselfish spirit that thinks ahead, goes beyond, and seeks to satisfy.

Caleb
Enthusiastic as Ever
from Joshua 14

The spies said there were giants. Caleb said there was a land to conquer. The spies felt like grasshoppers. Caleb felt like making them eat one. But in the end, he and his pal Joshua were the only two left standing after forty years in the wilderness. And Caleb wasn't finished yet.

Look at It This Way

There was a story told recently about a spunky Christian woman who died in her 90s. Only days before her death, however, she had sat down to map out her goals for the next ten years. That's an enthusiasm for life that death didn't defeat but only redirected.

If the Lord gives you long years, don't you hope you can keep that kind of enthusiasm into old age, never losing your spark, that hunger to do more, that fire to give God every ounce without regret?

First, a Quick Read

Now the men of Judah approached Joshua at Gilgal, and Caleb son of Jephunneh the Kenizzite said to him, . . . "I was forty years old when Moses the servant of the LORD sent me from Kadesh Barnea to explore the land. And I brought him back a report according to my convictions, but my brothers who went up with me made the hearts of the people melt with fear. . . . So on that day Moses swore to me, 'The land on which your feet have walked will be your inheritance and that of your children forever, because you have followed the LORD my God wholeheartedly.'

"Now then, just as the LORD promised, he has kept me alive for forty-five years since the time he said this to Moses, while Israel moved about in the desert. So here I am today, eighty-five years old! I am still as strong today as the day Moses sent me out; I'm just as vigorous to go out to battle now as I was then. Now give me this hill country that the LORD promised me that day. You yourself heard then that the Anakites were there and their cities were large and fortified, but, the LORD helping me, I will drive them out just as he said."

Joshua 14:6a, 7–8a, 9–12

When You Think about It

Caleb is a classic example of a man who never lost his spiritual edge. Where did this seasoned veteran get his spiritual grit—his *chutzpah?* What made him endure while others fell by the wayside right and left? The Bible says, "He followed the Lord, the God of Israel, wholeheartedly" (Josh. 14:14). Caleb never lost sight of the promises of God.

Interestingly enough, of all those who received the Promised Land as their inheritance, Caleb was the only one who completely drove out the enemy. He faced some of the most formidable foes in the entire land. Hebron was no garden spot. It was rugged and treacherous, containing a powerful enemy stronghold, guarded by the strongest men. It was no easy task to root out the enemy. But Caleb—even in his elderly years—was no lightweight. He wasn't looking for a pleasant retirement community to settle down in and rock his way toward heaven. He was looking for a scrap. He asked for one of the toughest assignments, and he successfully—single-handedly—drove out the enemies from Hebron.

While others longed for Egypt, Caleb longed for Hebron. While others looked back, Caleb looked forward.

—Greg Laurie

Wherever you are, be all there.

—Jim Elliot

> **CHARACTER CHECK**
>
> Seek out someone soon who's still modeling an enthusiastic Christian lifestyle into their older years. They'll inspire you to greater things. You'll inspire them to keep on going.

Phinehas
Righteous Indignation

from Numbers 25

Aaron could have learned a thing or two from his son, Phinehas. Faced with a similar outbreak of sin and rebellion among the Israelites, Aaron broke down under pressure. But Phinehas broke out. And his high regard for holiness gave the people a reason for hope.

Look at It This Way

Some things are worth fighting for. And our families are one of the biggest. The easiest targets are always the media and the movies. And certainly they carry their share of the blame. But some of the culprits come in much different cloaks. Like sixty-five-hour workweeks that run into months. And Saturdays at the golf course (ouch, that hurt). Even church meetings that take up three nights in a row. Sometimes you've got to put your foot down and say that your family needs you more than anyone else does. It's the right thing to do.

First, a Quick Read

While Israel was staying in Shittim, the men began to indulge in sexual immorality with Moabite women, who invited them to the sacrifices to their gods.

So Moses said to Israel's judges, "Each of you must put to death those of your men who have joined in worshiping the Baal of Peor."

Then an Israelite man brought to his family a Midianite woman right before the eyes of Moses and the whole assembly of Israel while they were weeping at the entrance to the Tent of Meeting. When Phinehas son of Eleazar, the son of Aaron, the priest, saw this, he left the assembly, took a spear in his hand and followed the Israelite into the tent. He drove the spear through both of them—through the Israelite and into the woman's body. Then the plague against the Israelites was stopped; but those who died in the plague numbered 24,000.

The LORD said to Moses, "Phinehas son of Eleazar, the son of Aaron, the priest, has turned my anger away from the Israelites; for he was as zealous as I am for my honor among them, so that in my zeal I did not put an end to them."

Numbers 25:1–2a, 5–11

When You Think about It

We have lost our spiritual equilibrium and inverted our values. We have ridiculed the absolute truth of Your Word and called it moral pluralism. We have worshiped other gods and called it multiculturalism. We have endorsed perversion and called it an alternative lifestyle. We have exploited the poor and called it the lottery. We have neglected the needy and called it self-preservation. We have rewarded laziness and called it welfare. We have killed our unborn and called it a choice. We have shot abortionists and called it justifiable. We have neglected to discipline our children and called it building their self-esteem. We have abused power and called it political savvy. We have coveted our neighbors' possessions and called it ambition. We have polluted the air with profanity and pornography and called it freedom of expression. We have ridiculed the time-honored values of our forefathers and called it enlightenment.

Search us, O God, and know our hearts today. Try us and see if there be some wicked way in us. Cleanse us from every sin and set us free.
—Joe Wright, in a prayer before the Kansas state legislature

A society that loses its sense of outrage is doomed to extinction.
—Chuck Colson

CHARACTER CHECK

It's easy to sit around decrying the ills of society. But when did you last stand up and do something constructive to fight evil, to champion the cause of righteousness?

Joshua
Filling Big Shoes

from Joshua 3 & 4

Moses was president, CEO, pastor, judge, and ruler all rolled into one. And his death literally took from the Hebrew people the only leader that generation had ever known. The task that lay ahead for his successor was more than impossible. Good thing it wasn't impossible for God.

LOOK AT IT THIS WAY

Even the most progressive of us still cringe at change. Your beloved pastor resigns to minister in another church. Or your boss—you'd finally gotten a good one—is transferred to another state. Just when you thought things were settled again, your widowed mother remarries or your favorite neighbors move away. And someone takes the place of someone who's irreplaceable. Turnovers like these are never easy, but if your trust is in God instead of in people, He can fill your seasons of change with unpredictable blessings.

First, a Quick Read

And the LORD said to Joshua, "Today I will begin to exalt you in the eyes of all Israel, so they may know that I am with you as I was with Moses. Tell the priests who carry the ark of the covenant: 'When you reach the edge of the Jordan's waters, go and stand in the river.'"

Joshua said to the Israelites, "Come here and listen to the words of the LORD your God. This is how you will know that the living God is among you and that he will certainly drive out before you the Canaanites, Hittites, Hivites, Perizzites, Girgashites, Amorites and Jebusites. See, the ark of the covenant of the Lord of all the earth will go into the Jordan ahead of you. Now then, choose twelve men from the tribes of Israel, one from each tribe. And as soon as the priests who carry the ark of the LORD—the Lord of all the earth—set foot in the Jordan, its waters flowing downstream will be cut off and stand up in a heap." . . .

That day the LORD exalted Joshua in the sight of all Israel; and they revered him all the days of his life, just as they had revered Moses.

Joshua 3:7–13; 4:14

When You Think about It

Think of the temptation Joshua must have faced. How easy it would have been to draw attention to himself and to attempt to build his own ego. Joshua, primarily because of his feelings of insecurity, was very vulnerable to this kind of temptation. Fearful people are vulnerable to pride. They often overreact to praise and honor. Their temptation toward self-exaltation is often greater than it is in people who are basically secure.

Joshua, however, did not respond either with false humility or with pride. He had discovered security in God's promises to him. He was able to rise above the temptation to glorify himself. He gave honor to the only One who could be given credit for the miracle that was about to take place.

Joshua's response was admirable, especially in view of the fact that he had been fearful and threatened by this great task. But his response shows the main reason why God chose to use Joshua in the first place. He knew He could trust him with this leadership role. He knew Joshua could handle the temptation that comes to every individual who is entrusted with great responsibility.

—Gene Getz

God hath work to do in this world, and to desert it because of difficulties and entanglements is to cast off His authority.

—John Owen

> **CHARACTER CHECK**
>
> Whether you're filling big shoes yourself or having to get used to someone who is, you're in one of God's most productive periods of testing. He'll see you through if you let Him.

Gideon
Fighting Doubts and Fears

from Judges 7

If all that comes to mind when you think of Gideon is a fierce fighting man, slamming clay pots and blowing trumpets, take a closer look at the material God chose to work with—a bundle of nerves whose fears left no doubt that victory came from —"the sword of the Lord."

Look at It This Way

Remember the fleece incident? Gideon stalls God for a sign—for something that makes him feel better about risking his life in battle, something a bit more substantial from God than just His word. And God graciously gives it. Not once, but twice.

God, of course, didn't owe Gideon anything. But He knew that this little tennis match he was playing wasn't some squinty-eyed —Prove it— born of raw, cynical skepticism. It came from someone simply scared to death of what the Lord was asking of him. And apparently, God's willing to work with that.

First, a Quick Read

Now the camp of Midian lay below him in the valley. During that night the LORD said to Gideon, "Get up, go down against the camp, because I am going to give it into your hands. If you are afraid to attack, go down to the camp with your servant Purah and listen to what they are saying. Afterward, you will be encouraged to attack the camp." So he and Purah his servant went down to the outposts of the camp....

Gideon arrived just as a man was telling a friend his dream.... "A round loaf of barley bread came tumbling into the Midianite camp. It struck the tent with such force that the tent overturned and collapsed."

His friend responded, "This can be nothing other than the sword of Gideon son of Joash, the Israelite. God has given the Midianites and the whole camp into his hands."

When Gideon heard the dream and its interpretation, he worshiped God. He returned to the camp of Israel and called out, "Get up! The LORD has given the Midianite camp into your hands."

"When I and all who are with me blow our trumpets, then from all around the camp blow yours and shout, 'For the LORD and for Gideon.'"

Judges 7:8b–11, 13–15, 18

When You Think about It

As it a sin to doubt? It can be if unbelief encourages disobedience to God or disloyalty to life's best. Yet doubt is not all bad. Some of history's notable doubters have become agents of change, correctors of error, and pioneers of new patterns of life. Great saints of the church, like Augustine and Luther, were plagued by periods of nagging doubt and depression. John Bunyan's classic allegory *Pilgrim's Progress* reports a Christian pilgrim's tortured victory over questions and severe trials. America was discovered by someone who disbelieved that the earth was square. There can be no greatness of devotion without the risk of defection from one's cause.

Faith and doubt, like joy and sorrow, together compose the life of God's people. Since commitment to Christ is a growing process, not a static experience, doubt may furnish an opportunity for growth. He learns through struggle to trust the dark. Personal experiences like betrayal of trust, fear of rejection, overwhelming tasks, and burdensome debts may provoke anxious concern in a stalwart heart. Doubt can destroy you. But if you learn to master it, skepticism can strengthen your Christian commitment.

—C. W. Brister

Every opportunity to fear is also an opportunity to trust God.

—John Maxwell

> **CHARACTER CHECK**
>
> Turn your fears and doubts into trusted warning signs that the challenge you're facing is too big for you to handle alone. God understands. He can help.

Jephthah
Speaking Careless Words

from Judges 11

Best case scenario: Jephthah just got a little carried away with himself, caught up in the nervous, battle-ready excitement around the Israelite campfire. Then why, after the way things turned out, would he go through with his rash promise? His was a bad case of foolishness.

Look at It This Way

In a world where nothing's sacred, God is still serious business. That's why even for believers, who feel no threat of eternal punishment, Christ's statement that "men will have to give an account on the day of judgment for every careless word they have spoken" is cause for caution and alarm (Matt. 12:36).

Our words matter. We toss them around so lightly, but their weight can be measured by the people they help or hurt, by the inner attitudes they reveal about us. May that day of judgment prove us people of careful words.

First, a Quick Read

Jephthah made a vow to the LORD: "If you give the Ammonites into my hands, whatever comes out of the door of my house to meet me when I return in triumph from the Ammonites will be the LORD's, and I will sacrifice it as a burnt offering."

Then Jephthah went over to fight the Ammonites, and the LORD gave them into his hands. He devastated twenty towns from Aroer to the vicinity of Minnith, as far as Abel Keramim. Thus Israel subdued Ammon.

When Jephthah returned to his home in Mizpah, who should come out to meet him but his daughter, dancing to the sound of tambourines! She was an only child. Except for her he had neither son nor daughter.

When he saw her, he tore his clothes and cried, "Oh! My daughter! You have made me miserable and wretched, because I have made a vow to the LORD that I cannot break." . . .

And he let her go for two months. She and the girls went into the hills and wept because she would never marry. After the two months, she returned to her father and he did to her as he had vowed.

Judges 11:30–35, 38b–39a

When You Think about It

Whatever the reasons behind Jephthah's rash vow, he paid for his actions—just as fathers throughout history have lost their children when vows at work conflict with vows at home. This story illustrated the double bind many men feel between the call of work and family. Many —warrior fathers— and men of integrity, zealous to uphold their work and their word at all costs, make the same mistake Jephthah did.

We can empathize with his dilemma by remembering that many fathers break promises to their family. We conveniently forget our girl's piano recital or our boy's baseball game for a "prior commitment" (another business meeting, a game of golf or a men's night out). Workaholics ask their family to understand that work must come first. Military men put "God and country" above family. So also Jephthah. He loved God and responded to the call of people who pressed him into military service . . . but forgot the welfare of his own family.

—Dietrich Gruen

Let your words be few, lest you say with your tongue what you will afterward repent with your heart.
—George MacDonald

CHARACTER CHECK

Like time, talents, and money, your words are a treasure to be managed with godly care and devotion. Always try putting some thought behind what you say.

Samson
Dealing with Consequences
from Judges 16

Samson blew it big time. Here's a guy with everything in the world going for him, and he throws it all away. For a thrill. For a kick. For a woman. But here's also living proof that even at the very end, even at the very bottom, people can change. And God can still hear.

Look at It This Way

Every picture you see of Samson is of this massive, hulking brute, carving up Philistines with a jawbone or snapping the city doors off their hinges. But if he were really some Mr. Universe look-alike, then why would his enemies have to resort to trickery to find the secret of his strength? If he were made out of muscle, then what's the big secret?

Samson knew that he was only as strong as his God let him be. How dangerous it is to see more in ourselves than is really there.

First, a Quick Read

Now the rulers of the Philistines assembled to offer a great sacrifice to Dagon their god and to celebrate, saying, "Our god has delivered Samson, our enemy, into our hands." . . .

While they were in high spirits, they shouted, "Bring out Samson to entertain us." So they called Samson out of the prison, and he performed for them.

When they stood him among the pillars, Samson said to the servant who held his hand, "Put me where I can feel the pillars that support the temple, so that I may lean against them." . . . Then Samson prayed to the LORD, "O Sovereign LORD, remember me. O God, please strengthen me just once more, and let me with one blow get revenge on the Philistines for my two eyes." Then Samson reached toward the two central pillars on which the temple stood. Bracing himself against them, his right hand on the one and his left hand on the other, Samson said, "Let me die with the Philistines!" Then he pushed with all his might, and down came the temple on the rulers and all the people in it. Thus he killed many more when he died than while he lived.

Judges 16:23, 25–26, 28–30

When You Think about It

The end of Samson's life is a solemn reminder that there are consequences to sin. For twenty years Samson assumed he could ignore all of the secret faults that lay beneath the surface of his life, but he was wrong. He thought he could get away with a few minor indiscretions from time to time, but he couldn't.

We all tend to believe at one time or another that we can ignore our sins. But the fact remains, our sins will not ignore us.

With his last burst of energy, Samson took hold of the pillars on either side of him. He was blind, but he had actually begun to see better than he had in more than twenty years. He heard the Philistines mocking God, so he prayed: "Oh Lord God, remember me and strengthen me just one more time." At long last, he realized that the strength he once possessed was not his, but God's. So he pleaded, "Let me die right here." With all of his great advantages thoroughly squandered, Samson finally began to understand: he surrendered his life completely to the will and purposes of Almighty God.

Better late than never.

—O. S. Hawkins

We do not need to fear that there is no place to return to after our fall.

—Augustine

> **CHARACTER CHECK**
>
> You may feel like you've made mistakes you'll never live down. But it's never too late to face your faults, learn your lessons, and do your best with what's left.

Boaz
A Case for Kindness
from Ruth 2

Old Testament men don't commonly come off as being kind. Their primitive habits and customs strike a noticeable contrast to the sensitive model of the modern man. Boaz was a big exception. His example of putting a priority on people still has a lot to say to us. Today.

First, a Quick Read

Ruth the Moabitess said to Naomi, "Let me go to the fields and pick up the leftover grain behind anyone in whose eyes I find favor."

As it turned out, she found herself working in a field belonging to Boaz, who was from the clan of Elimelech. . . .

So Boaz said to Ruth, "My daughter, listen to me. Don't go and glean in another field and don't go away from here. Stay here with my servant girls." . . .

She exclaimed, "Why have I found such favor in your eyes that you notice me—a foreigner?"

Boaz replied, "I've been told all about what you have done for your mother-in-law since the death of your husband—how you left your father and mother and your homeland and came to live with a people you did not know before. May the LORD repay you for what you have done. May you be richly rewarded by the LORD, the God of Israel, under whose wings you have come to take refuge."

"May I continue to find favor in your eyes, my lord," she said. "You have given me comfort and have spoken kindly to your servant—though I do not have the standing of one of your servant girls."

Ruth 2:2a, 3b, 8, 10b–13

LOOK AT IT THIS WAY

In reality, Boaz was much more than a kind, landed gentleman who gave Ruth the free run of his grain field. He was a kinsman-redeemer—one who by law had the right to buy the lands and possessions of bankrupt relatives in order to keep their holdings in the family.

In the same way, Jesus Christ is the one who has met us in our bankruptcy and assumed the role of our older brother, rescuing us from a debtor's prison by making full payment on our rising balance of sins, redeeming us from certain death.

When You Think about It

Clemens has his head full of imaginary piety. He is often proposing to himself what he would do if he had a great estate. He would outdo all charitable men that are gone before him; he would allow himself only necessaries, that widows and orphans, the sick and distressed, might find relief out of his estate. He tells you that all other ways of spending an estate is folly and madness.

Now, Clemens has at present a moderate estate, which he spends upon himself in the same vanities and indulgences as other people do. He might live upon one-third of his fortune and make the rest the support of the poor; but he does nothing of all this that is in his power, but pleases himself with what he would do if his power was greater.

Come to thy senses, Clemens. Make the best use of thy present state. Do now as thou thinkest thou would do with a great estate. Be sparing, deny thyself, abstain from all vanities, that the poor may be better maintained, and then thou art as charitable as thou canst be in any estate. Remember the poor widow's mite.
—William Law

Kindness is a sign of greatness.
—Lloyd John Ogilvie

Character Check

When you're tired, weighted down with personal matters or looming deadlines, that's when being kind to others is the hardest. It's also the time it looks best on you.

Samuel
Lifelong Obedience

from 1 Samuel 12

After a life spent in the spotlight, leading Israel through the difficult transition from the judges to kingly rule, Samuel presented himself to the people one last time—to right any wrongs, to make any amends. But the books were clear. He had been faithful for the long haul.

Look at It This Way

Samuel is one of a handful of Bible personalities we get to know from birth to death. We first meet him as a child in the Lord's house at Shiloh, learning to listen to God's voice. We see him painfully passing the baton to a weak-kneed wanna-be named Saul. We watch him giving his blessing to a shepherd boy with the heart of a king. In fact, we even catch a glimpse of him beyond the grave, conjured up by the witch of Endor. Yet from start to finish, from beginning to end, we find him 100 percent faithful.

First, a Quick Read

Samuel said to all Israel, "I have listened to everything you said to me and have set a king over you. Now you have a king as your leader. As for me, I am old and gray, and my sons are here with you. I have been your leader from my youth until this day. Here I stand. Testify against me in the presence of the LORD and his anointed. Whose ox have I taken? Whose donkey have I taken? Whom have I cheated? Whom have I oppressed? From whose hand have I accepted a bribe to make me shut my eyes? If I have done any of these, I will make it right."

"You have not cheated or oppressed us," they replied. "You have not taken anything from anyone's hand."

Samuel said to them, "The LORD is witness against you, and also his anointed is witness this day, that you have not found anything in my hand...."

"As for me, far be it from me that I should sin against the LORD by failing to pray for you. And I will teach you the way that is good and right.

"But be sure to fear the LORD and serve him faithfully with all your heart; consider what great things he has done for you."

1 Samuel 12:1–5a, 23–24

When You Think about It

One thing I would earnestly recommend to you who are afraid of backsliding and apostasy: Say to yourself: "Whether I get to Canaan or not, I will never go back to Egypt. I will die with my face toward God and holiness. Lord God, if I am cast away, if you never give me joy again, yet I will never cease to look to Your mercy in Christ Jesus, for there only have I hope. By Your grace I will die with my face to the cross." Did you ever hear of anybody who perished in that position? No. It shall never be reported in heaven above or in hell beneath that a soul died that way. No soul can perish whose eyes look toward the five wounds of Jesus crucified. He is the way, the living way, the only way, the sure way: Follow Him. Do as the blind man did who followed Jesus in the way: rise up now, for He calls you. Look to Jesus! Take this road of refuge, this way of grace. May God the Holy Spirit help you to take to the way at once, without delay!

—Charles Spurgeon

The virtuous man is that man who knowing that good thing to do, does that thing day after day after day.
—Thomas Aquinas

> **CHARACTER CHECK**
>
> The demands of righteousness sometimes seem so hard—too hard; but imagine being able to look back later with no regrets. Doesn't that sound worth it all?

Saul
A Loser at Leadership

from 1 Samuel 15

Saul has to go down in history as the biggest opportunity waster in all the Bible. Tall, handsome, brimming with potential, chosen by the Lord as Israel's very first king, filled full with the Spirit of God. The stuff of legends was his to write. But legends don't lack leadership.

LOOK AT IT THIS WAY

When you compare the sins of Saul with those of David, a confusing equation develops. David, as you know, didn't stop at adultery but turned his mistake into murder. Those are two biggies. All Saul really did to warrant God's anger was to offer a sacrifice out of turn and to bring an enemy king back alive—along with some sheep for burnt offerings. Minor violations? On the surface, maybe. But David melted before his accuser in sorrow and repentance. Saul met his accuser with excuses. His true colors were already starting to show.

First, a Quick Read

Early in the morning Samuel got up and went to meet Saul, but he was told, "Saul has gone to Carmel. There he has set up a monument in his own honor. . . ."

When Samuel reached him, Saul said, "The Lord bless you! I have carried out the Lord's instructions." . . .

. . . Samuel said, "Although you were once small in your own eyes, did you not become the head of the tribes of Israel? . . . Why did you not obey the LORD? Why did you pounce on the plunder and do evil in the eyes of the LORD?"

Then Saul said to Samuel, "I have sinned. I violated the LORD's command and your instructions. I was afraid of the people and so I gave in to them. Now I beg you, forgive my sin and come back with me, so that I may worship the LORD."

But Samuel said to him, "I will not go back with you. You have rejected the word of the LORD, and the LORD has rejected you as king over Israel!"

As Samuel turned to leave, Saul caught hold of the hem of his robe, and it tore. Samuel said to him, "The LORD has torn the kingdom of Israel from you today and has given it to one of your neighbors—to one better than you."

1 Samuel 15:12a, 13, 17a, 19, 24–28

When You Think about It

Great numbers of us, in all walks of life, do not live our lives in line with traditional standards for ethical conduct. Too many of us have embraced the modern-day, conditional approach to integrity. As a result, we too often capitulate to the virus of dishonesty and lower our standards for conduct. We too often take wrong action when the pressure is on in order to gain a false sense of personal advantage.

Moral immaturity is motivated by personal profit, prestige, or pleasure instead of intentionally deciding to do what's right. Compromising our character occurs when we underestimate evil and flirt with, and capitulate to, temptations of all kinds. Compromising our character is always just a choice away; it is enticed through flattery and fantasy. It ensnares us and brings about dishonest rationalizations and deceptions when we refuse to think about the rightness of our actions.

It is time for us to intentionally focus on God's proven values and principles for living and working. Then we will gain the maximum benefits of a balanced life and make this world a better place to live.

—Millard MacAdam

Those who rule must above all be able to rule themselves.
—Catherine of Siena

> **CHARACTER CHECK**
>
> Saul's biggest problem was not being able to admit he was wrong. Always be willing to face up to your mistakes, and never think your way is the only one.

Jonathan
A Friend to the End

from 1 Samuel 19 & 20

Jonathan and David had practically grown up together. Inseparable. But the years can change a friendship. And if Jonathan shared even a little of his father Saul's contempt, could David still trust him? Yes. Something in Jonathan's eyes made it clear. He was a friend for life.

LOOK AT IT THIS WAY

Friends are an important part of who we are. But the demands of marriage and family change the playing field of friendship, severing some of the spontaneity of single life.

That's why it's so important for husbands and wives to become friends—genuinely enjoying each other's company, looking for ways to be thoughtful, standing as a united front against the foes that threaten their commitment to each other, their family, their God. If you'll make your relationship top priority, the best friend you'll ever have is the one you married.

First, a Quick Read

Saul told his son Jonathan and all the attendants to kill David. But Jonathan was very fond of David. . . .

"Why should he be put to death? What has he done?" Jonathan asked his father. But Saul hurled his spear at him to kill him. Then Jonathan knew that his father intended to kill David.

In the morning Jonathan went out to the field for his meeting with David. He had a small boy with him, and he said to the boy, "Run and find the arrows I shoot." As the boy ran, he shot an arrow beyond him. . . . (The boy knew nothing of all this; only Jonathan and David knew.) Then Jonathan gave his weapons to the boy and said, "Go, carry them back to town."

After the boy had gone, David got up from the south side [of the stone] and bowed down before Jonathan three times, with his face to the ground. Then they kissed each other and wept together—but David wept the most.

Jonathan said to David, "Go in peace, for we have sworn friendship with each other in the name of the LORD, saying, 'The LORD is witness between you and me, and between your descendants and my descendants forever.'"

1 Samuel 19:1; 20:32–33, 35–36, 39–42a

When You Think about It

Not everyone is as blessed as these two men in connecting with a friend for life. I believe it is something most desire, but many—especially men—find it hard to attain. Madison Avenue realizes and acknowledges this. Just think about the way they choose to market products, such as beer. Beer commercials are directed, not so subtly, at men and promise two things: beautiful women and meaningful friendships with other guys who share a common gusto for life. The reason these guy-commercials are so designed is because the advertising agencies know men are looking for these kinds of relationships, but very few have them.

Perhaps Jonathan had looked all over Israel for a man who matched him in heart and mind. Perhaps he was as frustrated as some today because of the lack of meaningful friendships. But even though he was on the opposite end of the socioeconomic spectrum, as soon as he saw David, he instantly reached out in friendship. Jonathan and David had something very special, a relationship which became one of the most consistent and defining aspects of their lives.

—Jim Henry

A true friend unbosoms freely, advises justly, assists readily, adventures boldly, takes all patiently, defends courageously, and continues a friend unchangeably.

—William Penn

CHARACTER CHECK

The ground rules of friendship haven't changed since we were kids. To have a friend, be a friend. Be the kind of friend others can always count on. And you'll have a treasure for life.

David
Bigger Than Betrayal

from 1 Samuel 24

If anybody had good reason for putting a knife in Saul's back, it was David. But when David looked at Saul, he didn't see a man intent on killing him, didn't remember the spear coming straight for his neck. He saw the chosen of God. And that's all that mattered.

First, a Quick Read

After Saul returned from pursuing the Philistines, he was told, "David is in the Desert of En Gedi." So Saul took three thousand chosen men from all Israel and set out to look for David and his men near the Crags of the Wild Goats. . . .

A cave was there, and Saul went in to relieve himself. Then David crept up unnoticed and cut off a corner of Saul's robe.

Afterward, David was conscience-stricken . . . He said to his men, "The LORD forbid that I should do such a thing to my master, the LORD's anointed, or lift my hand against him; for he is the anointed of the LORD." . . .

Then David went out of the cave and called out to Saul, "My lord the king!" When Saul looked behind him, David bowed down and prostrated himself with his face to the ground. He said to Saul, "Why do you listen when men say, 'David is bent on harming you'? This day you have seen with your own eyes how the LORD gave you into my hands in the cave. Some urged me to kill you, but I spared you; I said, 'I will not lift my hand against my master, because he is the LORD's anointed.'"

1 Samuel 24:1–2, 3b, 4b, 5a, 6, 8–10

LOOK AT IT THIS WAY

David's godly restraint is reminiscent of another who would endure the blows of injustice, who would walk beneath his heavenly calling for a season in order to be obedient to God and submissive to His timetable.

The blood of David's royal line would one day soak a dirty hillside outside Jerusalem, pulsating from the hands, head, and feet of One with an unbelievable love for us—and an unbending respect for God's authority. Like David, no one could have faulted Him for taking the path of revenge. But only God's way brings a true reward.

When You Think about It

Though David followed God's principles in dealing with Saul in these two instances, he realized he could never fully trust the king again. This is apparent from David's behavior—and understandably so. When Saul invited David to come and be in his presence following the second encounter, David's reply was kind but negative. He had made his point with Saul—he did not return evil for evil—but he could not entrust his life to the king. Consequently, "David went on his way, and Saul returned home" (1 Sam. 26:25).

As Christians, we must forgive one another. I believe we are also to do everything we can to reestablish trust, even going the extra mile in reaching out to our enemies. However, there are times when it is no longer possible to trust another person totally. Like Saul, some people demonstrate again and again their untrustworthiness and unpredictable behavior.

David was saying he would never take Saul's life. However, he also was saying that the only one who could ultimately protect his life from Saul was the Lord. Never again would he trust the king.

—Gene Getz

You'll never regret forgiving someone who doesn't deserve it.
—Charles Swindoll

CHARACTER CHECK

Perhaps you've been treated unfairly, your rights trampled on. Retaliation surely seems like a solid option. But it's not the one God uses. Have you tried letting Him defend you?

David Uninhibited in His Worship

from 2 Samuel 6

Like all of us, David had trouble with a few things in his life. Worship wasn't one of them. Pain couldn't suppress it. Pleasure couldn't surpass it. In worship everything else took a distant second to pouring his heart, soul, and mind into exalting the name of his God.

Look at It This Way

Just a guess: When you hear the words *uninhibited worship,* you think of people swinging from the chandeliers, dancing in the aisles, jumping like jackrabbits. Not that we all couldn't use a taste of that from time to time, perhaps, but that's not what *uninhibited worship* is at all.

It can happen in the quietest of places, in the simplest of ways, when you lose all the worries about form and formality, when your love for God saturates your spirit—till worship ceases to be a drill and becomes a delight.

First, a Quick Read

David again brought together out of Israel chosen men, thirty thousand in all. He and all his men set out from Baalah of Judah to bring up from there the ark of God. . . .

David, wearing a linen ephod, danced before the LORD with all his might, while he and the entire house of Israel brought up the ark of the LORD with shouts and the sound of trumpets.

As the ark of the LORD was entering the City of David, Michal daughter of Saul watched from a window. And when she saw King David leaping and dancing before the LORD, she despised him in her heart. . . .

When David returned home to bless his household, Michal daughter of Saul came out to meet him and said, "How the king of Israel has distinguished himself today, disrobing in the sight of the slave girls of his servants as any vulgar fellow would."

David said to Michal, . . . "I will celebrate before the LORD. I will become even more undignified than this, and I will be humiliated in my own eyes. But by these slave girls you spoke of, I will be held in honor."

2 Samuel 6:1–2a, 14–16, 20–21, 14–16, 22

When You Think about It

When I stepped into the small, inviting chapel, I also stepped into my first experience with the liturgical. I wasn't accustomed to the worship environment—to the large table balancing the pulpit, to burning candles, to a worship leader dressed in vestments, to a guitar and folk songs mixed with an ancient chant and a classic hymn. I wasn't familiar with the kind of participation demanded of me—the dialogue, acclamation, and three Scripture readings punctuated by psalms, the bidding prayers, the passing of the peace, the personal touch of the priest calling me by name as he gave me the bread and wine, and the praise and celebration expressed in the Communion song.

You might say I was surprised by joy! I found myself ministering to God in praise, and God in turn was ministering to me. I had never had an experience like that in my life. A new worship experience had bumped up against an old prejudice of mine, and a new attitude was born. I had taken into myself the experience of another tradition, I had been in dialogue with another worship tradition, and I was surely the richer for it.

—Robert Webber

To worship is to quicken the conscience by the holiness of God, to open the heart to the love of God, and to devote the will to the purpose of God.

—William Temple

> **CHARACTER CHECK**
>
> Do it right now. Right where you are. Begin praising God. Out loud or in silence, till nothing else matters. We'll be doing it forever. Now's a great time to start loving it.

David Committed to Compassion

from 2 Samuel 9

King David, weary from constant demands on his time, finally gets a few minutes to himself. He sits down, takes a deep breath, and starts to think. About going to the beach? Winning his next battle? Would you believe inviting a poor cripple to come live in the palace?

Look at It This Way

Compassion is the quickest way to the heart of God. It's written all over the Bible, confirmed throughout ages of history, and verified by the deep feeling of rightness that caresses your spirit when you show kindness to someone who needs your help.

But it costs you. Maybe a lazy Sunday afternoon. Maybe a meal. Maybe a few hours of sleep. But it earns you a lot more than you give up. Hugs. Laughter. Joy. Respect. And a hunger to give even more, to care even more deeply, to be more like Christ, to love compassion.

First, a Quick Read

David asked, "Is there anyone still left of the house of Saul to whom I can show kindness for Jonathan's sake?" . . .

Ziba answered the king, "There is still a son of Jonathan; he is crippled in both feet." . . .

So King David had him brought from Lo Debar. . . .

"Don't be afraid," David said to him, "for I will surely show you kindness for the sake of your father Jonathan. I will restore to you all the land that belonged to your grandfather Saul, and you will always eat at my table."

Mephibosheth bowed down and said, "What is your servant, that you should notice a dead dog like me?"

Then the king summoned Ziba, Saul's servant, and said to him, "I have given your master's grandson everything that belonged to Saul and his family. You and your sons and your servants are to farm the land for him and bring in the crops, so that your master's grandson may be provided for." . . .

So Mephibosheth ate at David's table like one of the king's sons.

2 Samuel 9:1, 3b, 5a, 7–10a, 11b

When You Think about It

There is ingrained in the depths of human nature a dislike of the general ruck of mankind, in spite of all our modern jargon about loving humanity. We have a disparaging way of talking about the common crowd; though the common crowd is made up of innumerable editions of you and me.

Ask the Holy Spirit to enable your mind to brood for one moment on the value of the "nobody" to Jesus. The people who make up the common crowd are nobodies to me, but it is astonishing to find that it is the nobodies that Jesus Christ came to save.

The terms we use for men in the sense of their social position are nothing to Him. There is no room in Christianity, as Jesus Christ taught it, for philanthropic or social patronage. Jesus Christ never patronized anyone. He came straight down to where men live in order that the supreme gift He came to give might be theirs. It is only by getting our minds into the state of the mind of Jesus that we can understand how it is possible to fulfill the royal law and love our neighbor as ourselves.

—Oswald Chambers

I have come more and more to realize that being unwanted is the worst disease that any human being can experience.

—Mother Teresa

CHARACTER CHECK

Think of something sacrificial you can do this week, a way to show compassion to someone who can't pay you back, just for the joy of it. It's one of the purest acts of worship.

David
Ready to Repent
from 2 Samuel 12; 32 & 51

David never thought this day would come. He never would have believed he could fall so far, stoop so low. Nathan's words burned like an acid bath. "You are the man!" Rocked on his heels, hands to his chest, the real David returned. In repentance.

LOOK AT IT THIS WAY

There is confession. There is repentance. And there is a difference. David confessed, admitted his mistake. That's half the battle. But repentance is the tough part. Confession finishes its work in a moment. Repentance takes a lifetime.

Repentance means facing the same temptation again. And again. And again. And again. And saying no every time. And when you slip and say yes, it means getting back up—and saying no again. It's a painful path, a bruising battle, but every other road is a lie. Repentance is the only way home. Let's walk it together.

First, a Quick Read

The Lord sent Nathan to David. . . .
"This is what the Lord, the God of Israel, says: . . . 'Why did you despise the word of the Lord by doing what is evil in his eyes? You struck down Uriah the Hittite with the sword and took his wife to be your own.'" . . .
Then David said to Nathan, "I have sinned against the Lord."
2 Samuel 12:1a, 7a, 9a, 13a
When I kept silent,
    my bones wasted away
        through my groaning all day long.
For day and night
    your hand was heavy upon me;
my strength was sapped
    as in the heat of summer.
Then I acknowledged my sin to you
    and did not cover up my iniquity.
I said, "I will confess
    my transgressions to the Lord"—
and you forgave
    the guilt of my sin. . . .

Cleanse me with hyssop, and I will be clean;
> wash me, and I will be whiter than snow. . . .
Create in me a pure heart, O God,
> and renew a steadfast spirit within me. . . .
You do not delight in sacrifice, or I would bring it;
> you do not take pleasure in burnt offerings.
The sacrifices of God are a broken spirit;
> a broken and contrite heart,
> O God, you will not despise.

> Psalms 32:3–5; 51:7, 10, 16–17

When You Think about It

Sometimes, alas, sin even prevails over us, and we are forced in deep anguish to confess that we have fallen beneath its power. Who among us can say, "I am clean, I have not sinned"? Still, a temporary defeat is not sufficient to effect a total subjugation. Sin shall not have dominion over the believer, for though he falls, he shall rise again.

The child of God when he falls into the mire is like the sheep that gets up and escapes from the ditch as quickly as possible; it is not his nature to lie there. The ungodly man is like the hog that rolls in the filth and wallows in it with delight. The mire has dominion over the swine, but it has none over the sheep. With many bleatings and outcries, the sheep seeks the shepherd again, but not so the swine. Every child of God weeps, mourns, and bemoans his sin, and he hates it when for a while he has been overtaken by it. Sin has an awful power, but it has no dominion; it casts us down, but it cannot make us take delight in its evil.

—Charles Spurgeon

CHARACTER CHECK

Repent of it today. That sin. You know the one. That one that overtakes you no matter how fast you run. Satan will laugh, say you can't be trusted. He's right. But God can.

Repentance is but a kind of table-talk, till we see so much of the deformity of our inward nature as to be in some degree frightened and terrified at the sight of it.

—William Law

David
Accepting Disappointment
from 2 Samuel 7 & 1 Chronicles 17

No one loved to worship more than David did. Of the three kings who ruled over an undivided Israel, David stood head and shoulders above them all. If anyone deserved to oversee the building of the first temple, it was David. But it wasn't to be. And he took it like a man.

Look at It This Way

Life's not fair. We've all said it or thought it. We've all wished it weren't true. But it is. Life's not fair. Sorry.

But as believers in Jesus Christ, can't we all equally attest that our reward isn't fair either? Hope. Heaven. Forgiveness. Righteousness. Member in good standing in the glorious, eternal kingdom of God. To say we deserve far less is to not say it convincingly enough. Of all the unfair things in life, God's approving nod of grace toward us is the most unwarranted act of all. Hallelujah! Life's not fair!

First, a Quick Read

That night the word of God came to Nathan, saying:

"Go and tell my servant David, 'This is what the LORD says: You are not the one to build me a house to dwell in. . . .

"'When your days are over and you go to be with your fathers, I will raise up your offspring to succeed you, one of your own sons, and I will establish his kingdom. He is the one who will build a house for me, and I will establish his throne forever.'" . . .

Then King David went in and sat before the LORD, and he said:

"Who am I, O LORD God, and what is my family, that you have brought me this far? And as if this were not enough in your sight, O God, you have spoken about the future of the house of your servant. You have looked on me as though I were the most exalted of men, O LORD God.

"What more can David say to you for honoring your servant?". . .

"There is no one like you, O LORD, and there is no God but you, as we have heard with our own ears."

1 Chronicles 17:3–4, 11–12, 16–18a, 20

"Do as you promised, so that your name will be great forever. Then men will say, 'The LORD Almighty is God over Israel!'"

2 Samuel 7:25b–26a

When You Think about It

Do you have some cherished desire that you know you are going to have to relinquish? As we get older, many of us see that some of those great hopes and dreams are never going to be realized. Perhaps it is a dream of some great accomplishment through a unique kind of ministry. Maybe it is a desire for a certain kind of career or recognition. Maybe it is a desire for romance and marriage. Maybe it's a hope for relief from something in your life that you've had to live with for years. Whatever it is, you may now recognize that it is never going to happen, and that's a hard pill to swallow. But, like David, it's an opportunity to find satisfaction in what God has allowed you to do.

We can live the last years of our life swamped by guilt or overwhelmed by failures of the past. Or we can say, "By the grace of God, I did the best I could with what I had. And I claim His promise that somehow He'll use what I did accomplish for His greater glory."

—Charles Swindoll

The worth of life is not to be measured by its results in achievement or success, but solely by the motives of the heart and the efforts of one's will.

—George Seaver

> **CHARACTER CHECK**
>
> Have you had to face disappointment lately? In your job, your relationships, your health? No matter how down you may feel, God can get down beneath you. He'll keep you up.

David
Passing Down a Blessing

from 1 Chronicles 22 & 28

As quick on the trigger as David was, surely with his final words to Solomon had to search hard for breath between sniffles and sobs. But a lot of the pride was coming the other way, from a son who had seen these words lived, who had seen a good picture of God in his dad.

Look at It This Way

Blessings between parent and child don't have to be confined to the tearful drama of the deathbed. They can happen as you go, in the most casual, ordinary of circumstances. In enthusiastic cheers rained down from the bleachers. In words of forgiveness spoken to the top of their shame-heavy heads. In time carved out of your busy schedule especially for them. In a phone call out of the blue or a hand-written letter with a batch of homemade brownies. Blessings can be shared just about anywhere, appreciated just about anytime.

First, a Quick Read

David said to Solomon: . . .

"Now, my son, the Lord be with you, and may you have success and build the house of the Lord your God, as he said you would. May the Lord give you discretion and understanding when he puts you in command over Israel, so that you may keep the law of the Lord your God. Then you will have success if you are careful to observe the decrees and laws that the Lord gave to Moses for Israel. Be strong and courageous. Do not be afraid or discouraged. ". . .

"Now devote your heart and soul to seeking the Lord your God.". . .

"Acknowledge the God of your father, and serve him with wholehearted devotion and with a willing mind, for the Lord searches every heart and understands every motive behind the thoughts. If you seek him, he will be found by you; but if you forsake him, he will reject you forever.". . .

"Do not be afraid or discouraged, for the Lord God, my God, is with you. He will not fail you or forsake you until all the work for the service of the temple of the Lord is finished."

1 Chronicles 22:7a, 11–13, 19a; 28:9b, 20b

When You Think about It

When it comes to pictures about their future, children are literalists. For this reason, communicating a special future to a child is such an important part of giving the blessing. When a person feels in his heart that the future is hopeful and something to look forward to, it can greatly affect his attitude on life. In this way, we are providing our children, spouse, or friends with a clear light for their path in life.

Children begin to take steps down the positive pathway pictured for them when they hear words like these: "God has given you such a sensitive heart. I wouldn't be surprised if you end up helping a great many people when you grow older," or "You are such a good helper. When you grow up and marry someday, you're going to be such a help to your wife (or husband) and family."

We as parents cannot predict our children's future with biblical accuracy, but we can provide them with the hope and direction that is part of picturing meaningful goals. Our children can begin to live up to these goals and so will gain added security in an insecure world.

—Gary Smalley and John Trent

Like Joseph, we are foster fathers and foster mothers, charged with the caring of some of God's children while they live on earth and with preparing them for eternal life with their Father.

—Bert Ghezzi

> **CHARACTER CHECK**
>
> Make time to tell your children how proud you are of them, to share a verse that struck you in your quiet time, to let them know they've been on your mind. It'll bless their hearts.

David
Given to Good Stewardship

from 1 Chronicles 29

David closes his life preparing for something he'll never get to see—Israel's great house of worship, the temple he so longed to build. But even impending death couldn't dim his excitement for giving. He knew at seventy-one what he'd known all his life. Everything is God's.

LOOK AT IT THIS WAY

David possessed the visionary qualities of all great leaders: the ability to invest in things bigger than themselves, the drive to pursue goals and dreams laid up in store for future generations.

But putting that principle to work requires a sound perspective on godly stewardship. Before you can lose yourself in the big picture, you must first be willing to paint yourself out of it, to loosen your controlling grip on people and things, and let God perform His work with the resources He's given. It's His ball, His game, His field. But it's your call.

First, a Quick Read

They gave toward the work on the temple of God five thousand talents and ten thousand darics of gold, ten thousand talents of silver, eighteen thousand talents of bronze and a hundred thousand talents of iron....

David praised the LORD in the presence of the whole assembly, saying,

"But who am I, and who are my people, that we should be able to give as generously as this? Everything comes from you, and we have given you only what comes from your hand. We are aliens and strangers in your sight, as were all our forefathers. Our days on earth are like a shadow, without hope. O LORD our God, as for all this abundance that we have provided for building you a temple for your Holy Name, it comes from your hand, and all of it belongs to you. I know, my God, that you test the heart and are pleased with integrity. All these things have I given willingly and with honest intent. And now I have seen with joy how willingly your people who are here have given to you. O LORD, God of our fathers Abraham, Isaac and Israel, keep this desire in the hearts of your people forever, and keep their hearts loyal to you."

1 Chronicles 29:7, 10a, 14–18

When You Think about It

We don't own anything. God owns everything, and we are His managers. For most of us, the house we now call "my house" was called "my house" by someone else a few years ago. And a few years from now, someone else will call that house "my house." Do you own any land? A few years from now, someone else will be calling it "my land." We are just temporary stewards of things that belong to God. You probably believe that in theory already, but your giving will be a reflection of how much you genuinely believe it.

God has specifically said that He owns not just the things we possess, but even the money under our name in the bank and the currency in our wallets. So the question is not, How much of my money should I give to God? but rather How much of God's money should I keep for myself?

When we put a check or cash in the offering plate, we should give it with the belief that *all* we have belongs to God and with the commitment that we will use *all* of it as He wants.

—Donald Whitney

I have held many things in my hands and have lost them all; but whatever I have placed in God's hands, that I still possess.

—Martin Luther

CHARACTER CHECK

It's not easy to give. Until you start. So what are you waiting for? For blessings you'll never be able to contain, join the joyful army of the generous.

Solomon
Choosing Wisdom

from 1 Kings 3 & 2 Chronicles 1

It was the first time he had pondered this question in a dream state, maybe, but he'd done it many times before in his right mind. How in the world could he live up to the job of king? How could he follow an act like his father David? This was too big for one man.

LOOK AT IT THIS WAY

Knowledge is a microwave, serving up quick bits of information in five-minute bursts of news, traffic, and weather. It's a fast-food overload of the trivial and temporary, filling your head with bite-size chunks of processed facts.

But pursuing wisdom is like cooking with a Crock-Pot. It doesn't pop and sizzle. It doesn't glow red hot. And it won't be ready in ten minutes, even on its highest setting. But when the time is right, when all the spices and flavorings and juices have soaked through, you'll have something worth sharing. Something worth something.

First, a Quick Read

At Gibeon the LORD appeared to Solomon during the night in a dream, and God said, "Ask for whatever you want me to give you."
. . .
"Now, O LORD my God, you have made your servant king in place of my father David. But I am only a little child and do not know how to carry out my duties. Your servant is here among the people you have chosen, a great people, too numerous to count or number. So give your servant a discerning heart to govern your people and to distinguish between right and wrong. For who is able to govern this great people of yours?"

The Lord was pleased that Solomon had asked for this.
1 Kings 3:5, 7–10

God said to Solomon, "Since this is your heart's desire and you have not asked for wealth, riches or honor, nor for the death of your enemies, and since you have not asked for a long life but for wisdom and knowledge to govern my people over whom I have made you king, therefore wisdom and knowledge will be given you. And I will also give you wealth, riches and honor, such as no king who was before you ever had and none after you will have."

2 Chronicles 1:11–12

When You Think about It

The Hebrew word for wisdom refers to much more than an accumulation of facts. In the Old Testament, this word was used for anyone who had an unusual degree of skill in a given area. For instance, if a potter could create beautiful tableware, he was said to have wisdom. The word means to be skilled in some area of life. Wisdom in the book of Proverbs might be defined as the ability to live life skillfully from God's point of view. It comes from viewing life from a vertical perspective and acting accordingly.

Let no man think he will become wise by accident. No, a man must search after wisdom as if he were searching for silver or gold; he must set aside trivial pursuits in favor of that which comes only from God.

You must turn from evil if you really want wisdom. But there is a further step you must take. It involves humbling yourself, admitting your need, confessing your lack, and asking God to help you.

. . . If you want wisdom, you can have it. It's free, but it will cost all you have.

—Ray Pritchard

The business of the universe is to make such a fool of you that you will know yourself for one, and so begin to be wise.

—George MacDonald

> **CHARACTER CHECK**
>
> Wisdom takes time, moments of quiet reflection and thoughtful observation, and an open ear to God in prayer and Bible study. It won't happen overnight, but it will last over time.

Solomon
Turning Away
from 1 Kings 10 & 11

As it turned out, the wise man played the fool. Solomon found more to love in the treasures and pleasures of the world than he did in God. And yet for all his wealth, and all his women, he left behind a legacy of bitterness and emptiness. Hope it was worth it.

LOOK AT IT THIS WAY

Solomon's slippery slope into sin and self-destruction says a lot about the weight of our choices. For not only did his lust for life's delicacies cost him the favor of God and a lasting legacy of godliness, but it set in motion the entire collapse of the known Israelite world.

That's because choices never exist in a vacuum. And their consequences—whether for good or evil—compound over time. Each of us stands on the shoulders of choices made not only by us but also by others. It pays to make good ones, no matter how small.

First, a Quick Read

King Solomon was greater in riches and wisdom than all the other kings of the earth. . . .

King Solomon, however, loved many foreign women besides Pharaoh's daughter—Moabites, Ammonites, Edomites, Sidonians and Hittites. They were from nations about which the LORD had told the Israelites, "You must not intermarry with them, because they will surely turn your hearts after their gods." Nevertheless, Solomon held fast to them in love. . . .

As Solomon grew old, his wives turned his heart after other gods, and his heart was not fully devoted to the LORD his God, as the heart of David his father had been. He followed Ashtoreth the goddess of the Sidonians, and Molech the detestable god of the Ammonites. . . .

The LORD became angry with Solomon because his heart had turned away from the LORD, the God of Israel, who had appeared to him twice. Although he had forbidden Solomon to follow other gods, Solomon did not keep the LORD's command. So the LORD said to Solomon, "Since this is your attitude and you have not kept my covenant and my decrees, which I commanded you, I will most certainly tear the kingdom away from you and give it to one of your subordinates."

1 Kings 10:23; 11:1–2, 4–5, 9–11

When You Think about It

Christ said it was difficult for "the rich" to enter the Kingdom of Heaven, referring, no doubt, to "riches" in the ordinary sense. But I think it really covers riches in every sense—good fortune, health, popularity, and all the things one wants to have. All these things tend—just as money tends—to make you feel independent of God, because if you have them you are happy and already contented in this life. You don't want to turn away to anything more, and so you try to rest in a shadowy happiness as if it could last forever. But God wants to give you a real and eternal happiness. Consequently He may have to take all these "riches" away from you: if He doesn't, you will go on relying on them. It sounds cruel, doesn't it? But I am beginning to find out that what people call the "cruel" doctrines are really the kindest in the long run. If you think of this world as a place intended simply for our happiness, you find it quite intolerable: think of it as a place of training and correction and it is not so bad.
—C. S. Lewis

When a man ceases to worship God, he does not worship *nothing*. He worships *anything*.
—G. K. Chesterton

CHARACTER CHECK

The thought of turning away becomes more dull and distant the closer you get to Christ. Remind yourself often that you're in His presence. Remember that He didn't quit on you.

Rehoboam
In Bad Company

from 1 Kings 12

Old men for wisdom, young men for war. It's an adage as timeless as it is true, and those who trample on it get to learn their lessons the hard way. Solomon's son, Rehoboam—like those in each generation—got his chance to accept or reject it. He paid a youthful price.

First, a Quick Read

Rehoboam went to Shechem, for all the Israelites had gone there to make him king. . . . The whole assembly of Israel went to Rehoboam and said to him: "Your father put a heavy yoke on us, but now lighten the harsh labor and the heavy yoke he put on us, and we will serve you." . . .

Then King Rehoboam consulted the elders who had served his father Solomon during his lifetime. "How would you advise me to answer these people?" he asked.

They replied, "If today you will be a servant to these people and serve them and give them a favorable answer, they will always be your servants."

But Rehoboam rejected the advice the elders gave him and consulted the young men who had grown up with him and were serving him. He asked them, "What is your advice? How should we answer these people who say to me, 'Lighten the yoke your father put on us'?" . . .

He followed the advice of the young men and said, "My father made your yoke heavy; I will make it even heavier. My father scourged you with whips; I will scourge you with scorpions." . . .

So Israel has been in rebellion against the house of David to this day.

1 Kings 12:1, 3b–4, 6–9, 14, 19

LOOK AT IT THIS WAY

Our spiritual gut tells us we should associate freely with anyone, to not discriminate by holiness ratings. And that's basically true, as far as being a good in-the-world-not-of-the-world example of Christ's love and grace.

But the Bible's pretty clear about the distance we should keep from those who don't share our belief system. "Come out from them and be separate" (2 Cor. 6:17). "Have nothing to do with them" (2 Tim. 3:5b).

Serve everyone. Love everyone. But when it comes to close friends, guard your perimeter.

When You Think about It

It was an instance of Rehoboam's weakness that he did not prefer aged counselors, but had a better opinion of the young men that had grown up with him and with whom he was familiar.
Days should speak.

It was a folly for him to think that, because they had been his agreeable companions in the sports and pleasures of his youth, they were therefore fit to have the management of the affairs of his kingdom. Great wits have not always the most wisdom; nor are those to be relied on as our best friends that know how to make us merry, for that will not make us happy. It is of great consequence to young people, that are setting out in the world, whom they associate with, accommodate themselves to, and depend upon for advice. If they reckon those that feed their pride, gratify their vanity, and further them in their pleasures, their best friends, they are already marked for ruin. No more needs to be done to ruin men than to leave them to themselves, and their own pride and passion.

—Matthew Henry

Show me a man's companions, and I'll show you his character.
—Ed Cole

CHARACTER CHECK

Advice comes from all directions, in many forms, on lots of subjects. Make sure you have people around you whose advice you can trust. They're worth seeking out.

Asa
Confronting Family
from 2 Chronicles 14 & 15; Mark 10

Busting up altars to pagan gods and smashing the tools of their trickery was one of King Asa's most rewarding pursuits. He knew his cause was right, and he was ready to answer anyone who thought he was taking his religious purity too far. But what about Grandma?

Look at It This Way

Something takes over when we get around our families. We turn into children again. We become not who we are but who they see us to be. And to a degree, that's fine. It's wonderful to recapture a sense of the past, to retrace our steps with those who remember. But intensive care waiting rooms are coming. Late night phone calls are coming. Funeral homes are coming. And we'll wish we'd been mature enough to let God shine through our conversation. We'll wish we hadn't been so hesitant to share what's really important to us.

First, a Quick Read

Asa did what was good and right in the eyes of the LORD his God. He removed the foreign altars and the high places, smashed the sacred stones and cut down the Asherah poles. He commanded Judah to seek the LORD, the God of their fathers, and to obey his laws and commands. He removed the high places and incense altars in every town in Judah, and the kingdom was at peace under him. He built up the fortified cities of Judah, since the land was at peace. No one was at war with him during those years, for the LORD gave him rest. . . .

King Asa also deposed his grandmother Maacah from her position as queen mother, because she had made a repulsive Asherah pole. Asa cut the pole down, broke it up and burned it in the Kidron Valley.

2 Chronicles 14:2–6; 15:16–17

"I tell you the truth," Jesus replied, "no one who has left home or brothers or sisters or mother or father or children or fields for me and the gospel will fail to receive a hundred times as much in this present age (homes, brothers, sisters, mothers, children and fields—and with them, persecutions) and in the age to come, eternal life."

Mark 10:29–30

When You Think about It

One of the biggest reasons why most Christians tremble at the thought of witnessing to their own families is that those are the people who know them so well. They can smell the slightest hint of baloney on their breath.

Your family's need of Christ has nothing to do with what you have to offer, other than your total honesty about His grace and goodness toward you. What you want to show them is *His* worth. And the way to do that is to be truthful about His work in you, about your struggles as well as your successes.

You'll be a much more effective Christian just letting your loved ones see that you're still yourself or, more accurately, that you're *finally* yourself. Let them watch you in process, as you submit to the Holy Spirit's work in your life. Let them be inspired by a true artist at work, as He chisels away the stony facade of all that inherited sin and reveals the real, redeemable you.

They still won't see a perfect person. But you can let them see God's perfect work as He performs it in you.
—Jim Gilbert

Almost every day, we make decisions whether to heroically venture into people's lives and lead them to a place of spiritual safety, or to merely hope someone else will do it.
—Lee Strobel

> **CHARACTER CHECK**
>
> You're not called to be the judge of your family's faith. But you *are* called to demonstrate Christ's love to them and to stand up for His name even when it's unacceptable.

Ahab
Recognizing God's Power

from 1 Kings 21

Ahab was a scoundrel. No two ways about it. He and his wicked wife, Jezebel, thumbed their nose at God their whole life and made a mockery of Israel's throne. But there was a day when God got Ahab's attention—the day Ahab realized he wasn't the only king in town.

Look at It This Way

God was gracious to him, but we probably shouldn't interpret Ahab's actions as much more than fleeting humility. He died a coward on the battlefield, still resisting the word of the Lord. Ahab's melancholy merely proves that there are two kinds of sorrow a person can have over sin. "Godly sorrow brings repentance that leads to salvation and leaves no regret, but worldly sorrow brings death" (2 Cor. 7:10). For a moment Ahab felt sick enough to change his diet of deceit and debauchery. But that was before he dismissed it as just a bad case of heartburn.

First, a Quick Read

Then the word of the LORD came to Elijah the Tishbite: "Go down to meet Ahab king of Israel, who rules in Samaria. He is now in Naboth's vineyard, where he has gone to take possession of it. Say to him, 'This is what the LORD says: Have you not murdered a man and seized his property?' Then say to him, 'This is what the LORD says: In the place where dogs licked up Naboth's blood, dogs will lick up your blood—yes, yours!'"

Ahab said to Elijah, "So you have found me, my enemy!"

"I have found you," he answered, "because you have sold yourself to do evil in the eyes of the LORD. 'I am going to bring disaster on you. I will consume your descendants and cut off from Ahab every last male in Israel—slave or free.'"

When Ahab heard these words, he tore his clothes, put on sackcloth and fasted. He lay in sackcloth and went around meekly.

Then the word of the LORD came to Elijah the Tishbite: "Have you noticed how Ahab has humbled himself before me? Because he has humbled himself, I will not bring this disaster in his day, but I will bring it on his house in the days of his son."

1 Kings 21:17–21, 27–29

When You Think about It

Long ago, England was ruled by a king named Canute. Like many leaders and men of power, Canute was surrounded by people who were always praising him. Every time he walked into a room, the flattery began.

"So you say I am the greatest man in the world?" he asked them. "In that case, bring me my chair, and we will go down to the water." The men scurried to carry his chair over the sands.

"Sea," cried Canute, "I command you to come no further! Waves, stop your rolling! Surf, stop your pounding! Do not dare touch my feet!"

The tide came in, just as it always did. It came up around the king's chair, wetting not only his feet, but also his robe. "Well, my friends," Canute said, "it seems I do not have quite so much power as you would have me believe. Perhaps now you will remember there is only one King who is all-powerful, and it is he who rules the sea and holds the ocean in the hollow of his hand. I suggest you reserve your praises for him."

And some say Canute took off his crown soon afterward and never wore it again.

—James Baldwin

Only when man has restored his stolen throne to God are his works acceptable.

—A. W. Tozer

CHARACTER CHECK

Begin each day reminding yourself who's in charge of your life. It's always easier to ascribe power to Him rather than having it proven to you against your will.

Elijah
Dealing with Discouragement

from 1 Kings 19

Elijah was a rugged, woodsy, mountain man—a fiery Old Testament version of John the Baptist. But even a tough nut like Elijah could crack under the pressure of public opinion and the paralyzing fear of death threats. It was enough to make a guy question everything.

Look at It This Way

There's always a remnant—people who are not willing to blend into the world's fabric but are cut from a different cloth. They may never appear on the platform or be recognized for outstanding achievement. They just quietly, patiently, persistently, prayerfully put their trust in God—even when no one's looking.

Elijah hadn't seen them—seven thousand invisible people scattered along the streets, hillsides, and backwaters of Israel, whispering prayers of thanks and praise to God. Seven thousand! It's a wonder he hadn't noticed them, but not when all he could see were his own problems.

First, a Quick Read

Now Ahab told Jezebel everything Elijah had done and how he had killed all the prophets with the sword. So Jezebel sent a messenger to Elijah to say, "May the gods deal with me, be it ever so severely, if by this time tomorrow I do not make your life like that of one of them."

Elijah was afraid and ran for his life. When he came to Beersheba in Judah, he left his servant there, while he himself went a day's journey into the desert. He came to a broom tree, sat down under it and prayed that he might die. "I have had enough, LORD," he said. "Take my life; I am no better than my ancestors." . . .

And the word of the LORD came to him: "What are you doing here, Elijah?"

He replied, "I have been very zealous for the LORD God Almighty. The Israelites have rejected your covenant, broken down your altars, and put your prophets to death with the sword. I am the only one left, and now they are trying to kill me too." . . .

The LORD said to him, . . . "Yet I reserve seven thousand in Israel—all whose knees have not bowed down to Baal and all whose mouths have not kissed him."

1 Kings 19:1–4, 9b–10, 15a, 18

When You Think about It

Individuals in a drained condition feel caught up in a sea of feelings that often runs counter to all the facts. There are strong senses of self-doubt and negativism. The mind seeks out all the possible minor (and major) errors that might have been made in the past hours, and then it amplifies them until all positive contributions are mentally blocked out. Drained people become supercritical of self and, of course, of others. They are convinced they have made fools of themselves, that nothing done or said will be remembered or implemented.

When men and women are drained, they often generate moods that lead to their wanting to quit the tasks they've wanted to do the most. Like Elijah, they are convinced that their usefulness is over, that they are powerless to go any further.

The runner at Heartbreak Hill in Newton isn't surprised. He knows from experience and from the descriptions of others that he will feel exhausted and ready to quit as he plods along. And he doesn't quit because he knows what weariness is all about and where it comes from. The passion to finish the course and to win remains.
—Gordon MacDonald

No man ever sank under the burden of the day. It is when tomorrow's burden is added that the weight is more than a man can bear.
—George MacDonald

> **CHARACTER CHECK**
>
> It's natural to feel disillusioned at times—when people disappoint you, when troubles pile up. But God can give you supernatural faith to survive. Don't worry. You're not alone.

Elijah
Speaking Truth in High Places

from 2 Kings 1

It's one thing to express your indignant political opinions over dinner conversation. It's another to look straight into the eye of a world leader who could have your head at the snap of his fingers—and specifically outline his downfall. It takes more than guts. It takes God.

Look at It This Way

Ahaziah wasn't the only Israelite king to feel the heat of Elijah's indignation. Truly, the granddaddy of them all was Ahab, whose penchant for cultivating economic ties with neighboring nations had softened Israel's royal tolerance for pagan worship. And nothing got Elijah's dander up quicker than that. He was in his generation the conscience of Israel, and his faithfulness to stand up against blasphemy and injustice at the highest levels is a reminder that each of us has a responsibility to hold our leaders accountable for their actions and attitudes.

First, a Quick Read

Now Ahaziah had fallen through the lattice of his upper room in Samaria and injured himself. So he sent messengers, saying to them, "Go and consult Baal-Zebub, the god of Ekron, to see if I will recover from this injury."

But the angel of the LORD said to Elijah the Tishbite, "Go up and meet the messengers of the king of Samaria and ask them, 'Is it because there is no God in Israel that you are going off to consult Baal-Zebub, the god of Ekron?'" So Elijah went.

When the messengers returned to the king, he asked them, "Why have you come back?" "A man came to meet us," they replied. . . .

The king said, "That was Elijah the Tishbite."

Then he sent to Elijah a captain with his company of fifty men. . . . And said to him, "Man of God, the king says, 'Come down!'" . . .

The angel of the LORD said to Elijah, "Go down with him; do not be afraid of him." So Elijah got up and went down with him to the king.

He told the king, . . . "Because you have done this, you will never leave the bed you are lying on. You will certainly die!"

So he died, according to the word of the LORD that Elijah had spoken.

2 Kings 1:2–3, 4b, 5–6a, 8b–9a, 9c, 15–16a, 16c–17a

When You Think about It

Great Commission Christians make up slightly more than one-third of church members. They are participants. The rest are spectators. Participants choose battles of endurance, persecution, and mockery from the world's elite. Instead of taking the path of least resistance or bowing to political pressures, they arm themselves with God's Word. They stand on His principles and lay down their lives, reputations, and wealth for Christ. They are ready to turn the world right side up.

God didn't give you the armor listed in Ephesians 6:13–17 so you could sit on the bench and snooze. He wants you to go to war and fight for the cause of Christ and to establish His Kingdom on the earth. Are you man enough to step into the spiritual arena? Do you wilt when others mock you and sneer at your faith? Are you ready to pick up the sword of God's Word and fight with that weapon? Are you willing to put your reputation and image aside so you can leave a mark in the sands of time? If you are tired of lukewarm, minor league Christianity and want to enter the majors, the world awaits your influence.

—Tom Sirotnak

Well hast thou fought the better fight, who single hast maintained against revolted multitudes the cause of truth.

—John Milton

> **CHARACTER CHECK**
>
> You don't have to be a fist-pounding firebrand. But trust God for the boldness, the opportunities, and the wisdom to represent His cause well wherever He needs you.

JEHOSHAPHAT
Godly Governing

from 2 Chronicles 19

There are few bright spots among the kings who littered Israel's landscape between Solomon and the years of captivity. Jehoshaphat, however, is one of them. His high ideals for himself and his officials ring a patriotic cord in all of us who long for godly leadership in government.

First, a Quick Read

Jehoshaphat lived in Jerusalem, and he went out again among the people from Beersheba to the hill country of Ephraim and turned them back to the Lord, the God of their fathers. He appointed judges in the land, in each of the fortified cities of Judah. He told them, "Consider carefully what you do, because you are not judging for man but for the Lord, who is with you whenever you give a verdict. Now let the fear of the Lord be upon you. Judge carefully, for with the Lord our God there is no injustice or partiality or bribery." In Jerusalem also, Jehoshaphat appointed some of the Levites, priests and heads of Israelite families to administer the law of the Lord and to settle disputes. And they lived in Jerusalem. He gave them these orders: "You must serve faithfully and wholeheartedly in the fear of the Lord. In every case that comes before you from your fellow countrymen who live in the cities—whether bloodshed or other concerns of the law, commands, decrees or ordinances—you are to warn them not to sin against the Lord; otherwise his wrath will come on you and your brothers. Do this, and you will not sin."

2 Chronicles 19:4–10

LOOK AT IT THIS WAY

Of all the factors that led to Jehoshaphat's sound perspectives on government, perhaps the most distinct was his heritage. Jehoshaphat's desire to continue Asa's noble initiatives makes you think his father made an effort to do more than just leave behind a good example. You can almost imagine Asa, as his son became mature enough, bringing him into the decision rooms, discussing matters of loyalty and leadership on their twilight walks by the river. That's because heritage is a lot more than feats and accomplishments, but time and communication. We owe that to our children.

When You Think about It

Our laws and our institutions must necessarily be based upon and embody the teachings of the Redeemer of mankind. It is impossible that it should be otherwise; and in this sense and to this extent, our civilization and our institutions are emphatically Christian.

No purpose of action against religion can be imputed to any legislation, state or national, because this is a religious people. This is historically true. From the discovery of this continent to the present hour, there is a single voice making this affirmation.

There is no dissonance in these declarations. There is a universal language pervading them all, having one meaning; they affirm and reaffirm that this is a religious nation. These are not individual sayings, declarations of private persons: they are organic utterances; they speak the voice of the entire people.

The happiness of a people and the good order and preservation of civil government essentially depend upon piety, religion, and morality.

Religion, morality, and knowledge are necessary to good government, the preservation of liberty, and the happiness of mankind.
—United States Supreme Court, 1892

It is impossible to rightly govern the world without God and the Bible.
—George Washington

CHARACTER CHECK

Not many of us will hold governmental office, but you can pray for those who do and support those who use their positions to honor God with their actions and decisions.

Elisha
Modeling His Mentor

from 2 Kings 2

Elisha had felt God's call on his life. But Elijah gave that call a face. Whenever Elisha felt like quitting, like telling God he could never live this lonely life of a prophet, he'd see Elijah. He'd see all he ever wanted to be in life. And in the distance he could hear God's call again.

Look at It This Way

Basketball teams call him their go-to guy—the one whose track record proves he can deliver in clutch situations, the one whose attitude and desire raise the whole team's level of performance up a notch. That's what Elijah was for Elisha. He was his spiritual go-to guy. We all need rooted, godly people we can model our lives after, people who can share more over a cup of coffee than we get in a whole meal of our own ideas and perceptions. Aren't you hungry for that?

First, a Quick Read

When the LORD was about to take Elijah up to heaven in a whirlwind, Elijah and Elisha were on their way from Gilgal. Elijah said to Elisha, "Stay here; the LORD has sent me to Bethel."

But Elisha said, "As surely as the LORD lives and as you live, I will not leave you." So they went down to Bethel. . . .

Then Elijah said to him, "Stay here; the LORD has sent me to the Jordan."

And he replied, "As surely as the LORD lives and as you live, I will not leave you." So the two of them walked on.

Fifty men of the company of the prophets went and stood at a distance, facing the place where Elijah and Elisha had stopped at the Jordan. Elijah took his cloak, rolled it up and struck the water with it. The water divided to the right and to the left, and the two of them crossed over on dry ground.

When they had crossed, Elijah said to Elisha, "Tell me, what can I do for you before I am taken from you?"

"Let me inherit a double portion of your spirit," Elisha replied.

2 Kings 2:1–2, 6–9

When You Think about It

Every man should seek to have three individuals in his life.

You need a Paul. That is, you need an older man who is willing to build into your life. You need somebody who's been down the road. Somebody who's willing to share with you not only his strengths, but also his weaknesses.

You also need a Barnabas. That is, you need a soul brother, somebody who loves you, but is not impressed by you. Somebody who is not taken in by your charm and popularity and to whom you can be accountable.

Third, you need a Timothy. You need a younger man into whose life you are building. Paul spoke of the need for somebody who can affirm and encourage you, for somebody who will teach and pray for you, for somebody who will correct and direct you. That's the kind of person young people are looking for.

I can assure you after much experience that you haven't lived as a Christian until you have been mentored. And you haven't known fulfillment until you have been involved in the process of mentoring.
—Howard Hendricks

Attach a boy to a good man, and he seldom goes wrong.
—James Dobson

CHARACTER CHECK

Pray about finding a person who can hold you accountable and offer you encouragement, as well as a person who could benefit from your experience. It's a win-win situation.

ELISHA
Seeing with Spiritual Eyes

from 2 Kings 6

A prophet's work was life threatening. His task of articulating God's dead-steady message across the bow of public sentiment kept him constantly in the line of fire—from foe and countryman alike. But he had a weapon no enemy could calculate. Spiritual eyesight.

First, a Quick Read

Now the king of Aram was at war with Israel. After conferring with his officers, he said, "I will set up my camp in such and such a place."

The man of God sent word to the king of Israel: "Beware of passing that place." . . . Time and again Elisha warned the king. . . .

This enraged the king of Aram. . . . "Will you not tell me which of us is on the side of the king of Israel?"

"None of us, my lord the king," said one of his officers, "but Elisha, the prophet who is in Israel, tells the king of Israel the very words you speak in your bedroom."

"Go, find out where he is," the king ordered, "so I can send men and capture him."

When the servant of the man of God got up and went out early the next morning, an army with horses and chariots had surrounded the city. "Oh, my lord, what shall we do?" the servant asked.

"Those who are with us are more than those who are with them."

And Elisha prayed, "O LORD, open his eyes so he may see." Then the LORD opened the servant's eyes, and he looked and saw the hills full of horses and chariots of fire all around Elisha.

2 Kings 6:8–9a, 10b, 11–13a, 15, 16b–17

LOOK AT IT THIS WAY

Chances are, you use your spiritual eyesight even more than you realize. Not every spiritual inclination is Sunday morning testimony material, but that makes it no less valid. It may just be getting someone on your mind. Or reading God's fingerprint into a news event. Your sensibility to the Lord will grow, for sure, as you get closer to Him, spend more time in His Word— even more as you practice responding to His voice and expecting His direction. But you're doing it already. In fact, you're working on it right now.

When You Think about It

Ancient Israel and the early church both operated on the understanding that their weapons and abilities were not all material. They believed that they had at their disposal invisible, immaterial, supernatural forces.

The people of God in Scripture understood that we who do the work of God live in two worlds, the one we can see and the one we cannot. The modern Western church has come to believe itself limited to the same world as the unbeliever. We need the God of glory to open our eyes so that we can see beyond the limitations of our material world.

There is a time to cease rationalizing, to simply bow down before the awesome presence of the eternal God. We must regain piety in the good sense—a humble and wholesome attitude toward sacred things. And we must recover the sacraments—not just the perfunctory observance of them, but we need to learn to pass through them into the court of heaven. They should be windows in the wall of our material world through which we glimpse the glories of the world to come.

—Dan Scott

One of the hardest lessons we have to learn in life is to see the divine, the celestial, the pure, in the common, the near at hand.

—John Burroughs

CHARACTER CHECK

Part of the Christian walk is learning how to be quiet enough to listen to the Spirit's voice. Growth takes place in slow steps, by making mistakes, through prayer. And you can do it.

Uzziah
Pulled Down by Pride

from 2 Chronicles 26

Success is never enough for some people. Power, privilege—they blind people to their own limits. They render the attainment reflex uncontrollable. That was King Uzziah. He had success—God-given, God-blessed success. But he couldn't stop himself from wanting more.

Look at It This Way

Leprosy. The chalky white, emaciated skin. The worn nubs left behind by severed toes and fingers. The horrified, sideways glances from those who were so beneath Uzziah's kingly position. Could there have been a more fitting way to thoroughly pulverize his pride than to be stripped of his appearance, his freedom of movement, his place of honor—even to be too diseased for burial in the royal tombs, being laid to rest instead in a nearby field? Pride can blow a lot of air into your self-concept, but it offers nothing to brace your fall.

First, a Quick Read

Uzziah was sixteen years old when he became king, and he reigned in Jerusalem fifty-two years. . . . As long as he sought the LORD, God gave him success.

But after Uzziah became powerful, his pride led to his downfall. He was unfaithful to the LORD his God, and entered the temple of the LORD to burn incense on the altar of incense. Azariah the priest with eighty other courageous priests of the LORD followed him in. They confronted him and said, "It is not right for you, Uzziah, to burn incense to the LORD. That is for the priests, the descendants of Aaron, who have been consecrated to burn incense. Leave the sanctuary, for you have been unfaithful; and you will not be honored by the LORD God."

Uzziah, who had a censer in his hand ready to burn incense, became angry. While he was raging at the priests in their presence before the incense altar in the LORD's temple, leprosy broke out on his forehead. . . .

King Uzziah had leprosy until the day he died. He lived in a separate house—leprous, and excluded from the temple of the LORD.

2 Chronicles 26:3a, 5b, 16–19, 21a

When You Think about It

Uzziah knew the Scriptures. He knew that God's Law strictly forbade anyone to burn incense at that altar but one of the priests. He knew that he was violating the worship of God. But he had become blind. He couldn't even see the old familiar things he had known from childhood.

But that's what arrogance does. You begin to expect certain privileges in your life and feel angry or bitter when they don't fall your way. When you study the surrounding cultures of Uzziah's day, many of the other kings also had the privilege and prerogative of acting as priests. It may be that Uzziah looked around at some of the things his contemporaries were doing and thought, *Why can't I be a priest AND a king like these other guys? Are they better than I am?* Yet it was a direct violation of God's ways and God's commands. Uzziah knew it, but in his blindness he just couldn't see it anymore.

Uzziah started so well, lived up to so much of his potential, but finished out of the race. Why? Because he got suckered by pride.

—Steve Farrar

Pride leads to every other vice. It is the complete anti-God state of mind.

—C. S. Lewis

CHARACTER CHECK

Burn away your pride by continually yielding control of your thoughts, habits, and actions to God. Nothing in you will ever defeat it. That would only make you prouder.

Hezekiah
Powered by Prayer

from 2 Kings 19

Hezekiah knew kings weren't supposed to feel this way. But he was scared. To death. Sennacharib was coming, with an annihilating promise he had been known to fulfill. Sennacharib—just the name sounded like a fist in the stomach. Hezekiah's was already in a knot.

LOOK AT IT THIS WAY

Hezekiah's example offers one of the most descriptive word pictures in the vocabulary of prayer. The Bible says he took the warring king's threatening letter into the temple and "spread it out before the Lord." He knew this one was totally out of his control.

Perhaps that's why our deepest, most agonizing prayers drive us to a prostrate position. Face down on the floor. Arms outstretched. All vulnerabilities exposed. Empty-handed, with our bright ideas left behind. It's as low as we ever get before God. It's as close as we ever get to His heart.

First, a Quick Read

Now Sennacherib received a report that Tirhakah, the Cushite king [of Egypt], was marching out to fight against him. So he again sent messengers to Hezekiah with this word: "Say to Hezekiah king of Judah: Do not let the god you depend on deceive you when he says, 'Jerusalem will not be handed over to the king of Assyria.'" . . .

Hezekiah received the letter from the messengers and read it. Then he went up to the temple of the LORD and spread it out before the LORD. And Hezekiah prayed to the LORD: "O LORD, God of Israel, enthroned between the cherubim, you alone are God over all the kingdoms of the earth. You have made heaven and earth. Give ear, O LORD, and hear; open your eyes, O LORD, and see; listen to the words Sennacherib has sent to insult the living God. . . .

"Now, O LORD our God, deliver us from his hand, so that all kingdoms on earth may know that you alone, O LORD, are God." . . .

That night the angel of the LORD went out and put to death a hundred and eighty-five thousand men in the Assyrian camp.

2 Kings 19:9–10, 14–16, 19, 35a

When You Think about It

They had encountered a very dense fog. Because of it, the captain had remained on the bridge continuously for twenty-four hours when George Mueller came to him and said, "Captain, I have come to tell you that I must be in Quebec on Saturday afternoon." When he was informed that it was impossible, he replied, "Very well, if the ship cannot take me, God will find some other way. Let us go down to the chart room and pray."

"'Mr. Mueller,' I said, 'do you not know how dense the fog is?' 'No,' he replied. 'My eye is not on the density of the fog, but on the Living God who controls every circumstance of my life.' He knelt down and prayed a simple prayer. I looked at him, and he said, 'Get up and open the door and you will find that the fog is gone.'"

I got up, and indeed the fog was gone. George Mueller was in Quebec Saturday afternoon for his engagement. I learned from that man that if you know God and if you know His will for your life, and circumstances seem impossible, pray believing that God will—and He will!"

—Norman Harrison

The ceremony of lifting up our hands in prayer is designed to remind us that we are far removed from God, unless our thoughts rise upward.

—John Calvin

CHARACTER CHECK

When's the last time you cried out to God—when you spread everything out before Him and totally submitted to His will? There's rest and release waiting down on the carpet.

Josiah
Renewing the Covenant

from 2 Chronicles 34

It had been years since Israelite families had celebrated their prescribed feasts or united in worship to something besides a carved rock or a piece of wood. God's distinguishing marks were all but gone from His people—till one king found a light in the dark ages.

LOOK AT IT THIS WAY

Some historians cast a skeptical eye on this event in Israel's history. They propose that Josiah was coerced by the priests to go along with this scheme of "finding" (wink, wink) a divinely written scroll, thus throwing the weight of God behind their programs of reinvigorating national morality.

There will always be those who cast doubt on the Bible, who roll their eyes at God's people and explain away His work. You're not likely to convince them by argument. But if they'll only believe what they see, let them see a faithful follower in you.

First, a Quick Read

In the eighteenth year of Josiah's reign, to purify the land and the temple, he sent Shaphan son of Azaliah and Maaseiah the ruler of the city, with Joah son of Joahaz, the recorder, to repair the temple of the LORD his God. . . .

While they were bringing out the money that had been taken into the temple of the LORD, Hilkiah the priest found the Book of the Law of the LORD that had been given through Moses. . . .

When the king heard the words of the Law, he tore his robes. . . .

Then the king called together all the elders of Judah and Jerusalem. He went up to the temple of the LORD with the men of Judah, the people of Jerusalem, the priests and the Levites—all the people from the least to the greatest. He read in their hearing all the words of the Book of the Covenant, which had been found in the temple of the LORD. The king stood by his pillar and renewed the covenant in the presence of the LORD—to follow the LORD and keep his commands, regulations and decrees with all his heart and all his soul, and to obey the words of the covenant written in this book.

2 Chronicles 34:8, 14, 19, 29–31

When You Think about It

If you want to begin praying for revival in the nation, start by seeking revival in your own heart, and let revival begin in you.

Our only hope for a future in our nation is for revival to sweep our churches and spiritual awakening to touch the land. If our nation is to return to the Lord and fear Him once again, God's people must begin the repentance.

We must meet God's requirements. We must deal ruthlessly with our stubborn pride, and humble ourselves before the Lord. Then we must pray and seek His face. Prayer is a relationship with a person. Prayer is entering into the throne room of the universe to stand before the Lord God Almighty. When God's people take prayer seriously and enter the presence of Holy God, they will recognize their sin, and fall with broken and contrite hearts before His majesty.

When we come to understand the nature of our sin, and when we have a broken heart about it, we will be ready to repent and return to the Lord. God stands ready to grant and enable our repentance, if we will just respond to His invitation.

—Henry Blackaby

God cannot sustain this free and blessed country, which we love and pray for, unless the church will take right ground.

—Charles Finney

> **CHARACTER CHECK**
>
> Right now might be a good time in life for you to stop and think—to see how close you're walking to the truths you profess. Renew your priorities in light of God's Word.

Ezra
A Love for God's Word

from Ezra 7; Nehemiah 7 & 8

With a Bible in every room, we have no way of understanding how precious that scroll was to Ezra. We probably don't even have a way to feel the full weight of those precious words in the same way he did. When he read them, everyone knew he was doing what he loved.

Look at It This Way

Have you ever heard of someone tell how, from fatigue or some disorientation, they were driving in their car, arrived at their destination, and suddenly realized they had no recollection of the trip? Is that the way Bible reading has become for you? You sit down, you start off a chapter, then you look up five minutes later with no idea what you've just read?

Try Ezra's way. Try reading the Bible aloud next time, adding your ears as a member of the audience, and see if you don't enjoy the ride a lot more.

First, a Quick Read

Ezra arrived in Jerusalem in the fifth month of the seventh year of the king. He had begun his journey from Babylon on the first day of the first month, and he arrived in Jerusalem on the first day of the fifth month, for the gracious hand of his God was on him. For Ezra had devoted himself to the study and observance of the Law of the LORD, and to teaching its decrees and laws in Israel.

Ezra 7:8–10

When the seventh month came and the Israelites had settled in their towns, all the people assembled as one man in the square before the Water Gate. They told Ezra the scribe to bring out the Book of the Law of Moses, which the LORD had commanded for Israel.

So on the first day of the seventh month, Ezra the priest brought the Law before the assembly, which was made up of men and women and all who were able to understand.

He read it aloud from daybreak till noon as he faced the square before the Water Gate in the presence of the men, women and others who could understand. And all the people listened attentively to the Book of the Law.

Nehemiah 7:73b–8:3

When You Think about It

Living among the Chaldeans, who were famous for the study of literature and astronomy, perhaps made it difficult for Ezra to prefer to study the law of the Lord. But he sought the law of the Lord; he made it his business to search the Scriptures and to inquire into the knowledge of God. He knew that he could find the knowledge and the will of God in the Scriptures, but he also knew that he would not find it without seeking for it. So he prepared his heart to do it; he took pains in his studies; and he became a ready scribe.

After being instrumental in reviving the knowledge of God among the captive Jews in Babylon, Ezra went to Jerusalem to teach Israel. He offered "to teach in Israel the statutes and judgments" of God's law, for he was willing to share what he had learned for the good of others. You will observe, however, that he first learned and then taught; he first practiced the commandments himself and then directed others in the practice of them. His example confirmed his doctrine.
—Matthew Henry

The Bible is alive, it speaks to me; it has feet, it runs after me; it has hands, it lays hold of me.
—Martin Luther

> **CHARACTER CHECK**
>
> Love for God's Word is only found in God's Word—as you read it and study it with more faithfulness than any other book or attraction. Mark it down. And do it every day.

Nehemiah Unpolluted by Power

from Nehemiah 5

Nehemiah was in charge, which meant that all the privileges of power were his to enjoy. But he had learned a concept Jesus would later put into words. "Whoever wants to be first must be slave of all" (Mark 10:44). Nehemiah would join Him in putting it into practice.

Look at It This Way

Write it down. This is just God's way. Those who are seeking His will for their lives, and who find it in noticeable positions of prominence, are those He's been able to trust with the ordinary and obscure. The principle that Christ taught in the parable of the talents will always hold true. "You have been faithful with a few things; I will put you in charge of many things" (Matt. 25:21). If we'll concentrate on doing well what is right in front of us, God will open the door to fulfillment when we're ready for it.

First, a Quick Read

Moreover, from the twentieth year of King Artaxerxes, when I was appointed to be their governor in the land of Judah, until his thirty-second year—twelve years—neither I nor my brothers ate the food allotted to the governor. But the earlier governors—those preceding me—placed a heavy burden on the people and took forty shekels of silver from them in addition to food and wine. Their assistants also lorded it over the people. But out of reverence for God I did not act like that. Instead, I devoted myself to the work on this wall. All my men were assembled there for the work; we did not acquire any land.

Furthermore, a hundred and fifty Jews and officials ate at my table, as well as those who came to us from the surrounding nations. Each day one ox, six choice sheep and some poultry were prepared for me, and every ten days an abundant supply of wine of all kinds. In spite of all this, I never demanded the food allotted to the governor, because the demands were heavy on these people.

Remember me with favor, O my God, for all I have done for these people.

Nehemiah 5:14–19

When You Think about It

Nehemiah was motivated by three factors as he carried out his work as governor. He feared God, he was sensitive to people's needs, and he desired God's special blessing in his life. If we approach advancement and promotion with these same basic motivations, we, too, will have the key to maintaining our spiritual and psychological equilibrium.

Today, we need more godly fear. Rightly defined, this means we should stand in awe of who God is and what He's done for us—and that eventually we will have to give an account to Him for how we have lived our lives on earth.

If as Christians we are sensitive to others, we'll not take advantage of them. We'll never use our positions of power to exploit people. Rather, we'll use these opportunities to help people—to make their lives more comfortable and to create better living and working conditions. Our goal will be like that of Christ—to become a greater servant as our position of authority and power increases. When we are motivated by this kind of thinking, I'm convinced we'll be able to handle almost any promotion without succumbing to Satan's tactics.

—Gene Getz

Adversity is hard on a man; but for one man who can stand prosperity, there are a hundred that will stand adversity.

—Thomas Carlyle

> **CHARACTER CHECK**
>
> Even the seduction of power can't fool you when your heart is fixed on pleasing the Lord. Be a person who's not as worried about what you deserve as Who you serve.

Mordecai
Advocate for the Oppressed

from Esther 3 & 4

If you want to find Mordecai in the story of Esther, look for him out in the street—with one ear on his people's concerns and the other on the rumors streaming from the palace—rumors of a plot to destroy them. With Mordecai, the Jewish people had a fighting chance.

LOOK AT IT THIS WAY

Isaiah 58 is one of the Bible's most probing examinations of the believer's heart. Speaking God's words, the prophet takes on the proud proponents of religious observance—those who are so certain God couldn't be more pleased with their ritual and righteousness. Isaiah pleads with them to see what should be so obvious—that going without food means little while the oppressed go hungry, that wearing sackcloth only makes you itchy if the naked around you remain unclothed. God's heart is for the helpless, and His people don't really know Him if they aren't actively helping them.

First, a Quick Read

Then Haman said to King Xerxes, "There is a certain people dispersed and scattered among the peoples in all the provinces of your kingdom whose customs are different from those of all other people and who do not obey the king's laws; it is not in the king's best interest to tolerate them. If it pleases the king, let a decree be issued to destroy them, and I will put ten thousand talents of silver into the royal treasury for the men who carry out this business." . . .

When Mordecai learned of all that had been done, he tore his clothes, put on sackcloth and ashes, and went out into the city, wailing loudly and bitterly.

So Hathach went out to Mordecai in the open square of the city in front of the king's gate. Mordecai told him everything that had happened to him, including the exact amount of money Haman had promised to pay into the royal treasury for the destruction of the Jews. He also gave him a copy of the text of the edict for their annihilation, which had been published in Susa, to show to Esther and explain it to her, and he told him to urge her to go into the king's presence to beg for mercy and plead with him for her people.

Esther 3:8–9; 4:1, 6–8

When You Think about It

Cultures can be judged in many ways, but eventually every nation in every age must be judged by this test: *how did it treat people?*

The great dramatic moments of history have left us with monuments and memories of compassion, love, and unselfishness which punctuate the all-too-pervasive malevolence that dominates so much of human interaction. That there is any respite from evil is due to some courageous people who, on the basis of personal philosophies, have led campaigns against the ill-treatment and misuse of individuals. Each era faces its own unique blend of problems. Our own time is no exception. Those who regard individuals as expendable raw material—to be molded, exploited, and then discarded—do battle on many fronts with those who see each person as unique and special, worthwhile, and irreplaceable.

There are choices to be made in every age. And who we are depends on the choices we make. What will our choices be? What boundaries will we uphold to make it possible for people to say with certainty that moral atrocities are truly evil? Which side will we be on?

—Francis Schaeffer

God measures societies by what they do to the weakest and poorest.
—Ron Sider

> **CHARACTER CHECK**
>
> You can't champion every cause, but you can visit a nursing home. You can write a letter. You can skip a meal and feed a beggar. Don't wait for another guilt trip. Catch this one.

Haman
A Prisoner to Prejudice

from Esther 3 & 5

Haman didn't just say the word *Jew*. He spit it. It came out with a venom his heart couldn't contain. They were pests. They were appalling. They were in his way. And he was going to rid his land of them if it was the last thing he did. But he had to leave his plans hanging.

Look at It This Way

Do you know the rest of the story? The gallows that Haman had built for Mordecai would feel the weight of his own hate instead. But isn't that always the way with prejudice? Those who possess its poison inside are the ones who really suffer. It breaks down their relationships, distorts their perspectives, and stands like a stiff-arm between them and God. And in trying to justify their principles of prejudice, they come off looking as foolish as Haman did, falling all over himself on his way to a fool's grave.

First, a Quick Read

All the royal officials at the king's gate knelt down and paid honor to Haman, for the king had commanded this concerning him. But Mordecai would not kneel down or pay him honor. . . .

When Haman saw that Mordecai would not kneel down or pay him honor, he was enraged. Yet having learned who Mordecai's people were, he scorned the idea of killing only Mordecai. Instead Haman looked for a way to destroy all Mordecai's people, the Jews, throughout the whole kingdom of Xerxes. . . .

Calling together his friends and Zeresh, his wife, Haman boasted to them about his vast wealth, his many sons, and all the ways the king had honored him and how he had elevated him above the other nobles and officials. . . . "But all this gives me no satisfaction as long as I see that Jew Mordecai sitting at the king's gate."

His wife Zeresh and all his friends said to him, "Have a gallows built, seventy-five feet high, and ask the king in the morning to have Mordecai hanged on it." . . . This suggestion delighted Haman, and he had the gallows built.

Esther 3:2, 5–6; 5:10b–11, 13–14

When You Think about It

The first thing that happens after we have realized our election to God in Christ Jesus is the destruction of our prejudices and our parochial notions and our patriotisms; we are turned into servants of God's own purpose.

Our Lord never nurses our prejudices. He mortifies them, runs clean athwart them. We imagine that God has a special interest in our particular prejudices; we are quite sure that God will never deal with us as He has to deal with other people.

Instead of God being on the side of our prejudices, He is deliberately wiping them out. It is part of our moral education to have our prejudices run straight across by His providence. God pays no respect to anything we bring to Him. There is only one thing God wants of us, and that is our unconditional surrender.

When once we realize that through the salvation of Jesus Christ we are made perfectly fit for God, we shall understand why Jesus Christ is so ruthless in His demands. He demands absolute rectitude from His servants, because He has put into them the very nature of God.
—Oswald Chambers

Our problem in this nation isn't a skin problem; it's a sin problem.
—Wellington Boone

> **CHARACTER CHECK**
>
> Even in its small, acceptable forms in society, prejudice leaves bites that can sting for a long time. Ask yourself a hard question. Is there prejudice inside? And another one. Why?

Job
Faith That Perseveres
from Job 16 & 19

Job's patience is legendary. Even those who give little thought to the things of God know a little of his story. But those who know better can hang around long enough to see more than the patience of Job. They'll see that perseverance is pointless unless your hope has a Name.

LOOK AT IT THIS WAY

When you're going through a difficult time, it's nice to have friends. Unless, of course, your friends are like Job's. But even with all their pious ramblings, who knows how much harder it would have been on Job if he'd had to endure his trial alone? At least they were there. His other friends didn't even show.

Sometimes you may stop short of reaching out to someone who's hurting, not sure what to say or how to show your concern. But almost always, it's not your words but just your presence that does the caring.

First, a Quick Read

God has turned me over to evil men
 and thrown me into the clutches of the wicked.
All was well with me, but he shattered me;
 he seized me by the neck and crushed me.
He has made me his target;
 his archers surround me.
Without pity, he pierces my kidneys
 and spills my gall on the ground.
Again and again he bursts upon me;
 he rushes at me like a warrior. . . .
My face is red with weeping,
 deep shadows ring my eyes;
yet my hands have been free of violence
 and my prayer is pure. . . .
Even now my witness is in heaven;
 my advocate is on high.
My intercessor is my friend
 as my eyes pour out tears to God;
on behalf of a man he pleads with God
 as a man pleads for his friend. . . .

> I know that my Redeemer lives,
>   and that in the end he will stand upon the earth.
> And after my skin has been destroyed,
>   yet in my flesh I will see God;
> I myself will see him
>   with my own eyes—I, and not another.
>   How my heart yearns within me!
>
> Job 16:11–14, 16–17, 19–21; 19:25–27

When You Think about It

"Thou hast enlarged me when I was in distress" (Ps. 4:1). The more one thinks of these words, the more they reveal their wonderful meaning. Darby renders it, "In pressure, Thou hast enlarged me," and Kay, "In straits Thou madest wide room for me." Whatever the pressure be, in that pressure—think of it—enlargement; the very opposite of what the word "pressure" suggests. And room, plenty of room, in a strait place.

We may sometimes feel distressed: here then is a word of pure hope and consolation. Largeness, like the largeness of the sea, is His gift to us. We shall not be flattened in spirit by pressure, but enlarged. In the narrow ways of pain or of temptation, He will make wide room for us.

In Job's deepest despondency, he wished to be as he was when "the intimacy of God was over [his] tent" (Job 29:4), and he did not know that, even then, he was very near to a more wonderful intimacy than had ever been his before. Is it not joyful to think that it may be so with us?

Today, even today, we may be on the verge of—what?

—Amy Carmichael

> **CHARACTER CHECK**
>
> There are times when, even with all the Bible words in the world, there's no answer for what you're facing. Except one.
> *Jesus.* Cling to Him. He's the only hope you've got.

Great works are performed, not by strength, but by perseverance.

—Samuel Johnson

Isaiah
Fearing God
from Isaiah 6

You've heard this passage preached time and time again. But no matter how many approaches you take, one thing is unmistakable. Isaiah saw something awesome. Awesome's not your kind of word? Then numbing, staggering, breathtaking. Feel it again.

First, a Quick Read

In the year that King Uzziah died, I saw the Lord seated on a throne, high and exalted, and the train of his robe filled the temple. Above him were seraphs, each with six wings: With two wings they covered their faces, with two they covered their feet, and with two they were flying. And they were calling to one another:

"Holy, holy, holy is the LORD Almighty;
    the whole earth is full of his glory."

At the sound of their voices the doorposts and thresholds shook and the temple was filled with smoke.

"Woe to me!" I cried. "I am ruined! For I am a man of unclean lips, and I live among a people of unclean lips, and my eyes have seen the King, the LORD Almighty."

Then one of the seraphs flew to me with a live coal in his hand, which he had taken with tongs from the altar. With it he touched my mouth and said, "See, this has touched your lips; your guilt is taken away and your sin atoned for."

Then I heard the voice of the Lord saying, "Whom shall I send? And who will go for us?"

And I said, "Here am I. Send me!"

Isaiah 6:1–8

LOOK AT IT THIS WAY

Uzziah had been king for what seemed like forever. Longer than any other person in Jewish history—fifty-two years, from age sixteen to age seventy-eight. He was certainly the only king that Isaiah had ever known. And his death—no matter how expected at such an advanced age—had to rattle a deep chord of disbelief. Uzziah, dead. It seemed impossible.

That had to be Isaiah's mood the day God shuddered him to his socks with the painful brilliance of His presence. When everything stable had suddenly been shaken, God gave Isaiah a glimpse of the unshakable. And he never forgot it.

When You Think about It

On olden days, men of faith were said to "walk in the fear of God." However intimate their communion with God, however bold their prayers, at the base of their religious life was the conception of God as awesome and dreadful. The idea of God transcendent runs through the whole Bible and gives color and tone to the character of the saints.

Whenever God appeared to men in Bible times, the results were the same—an overwhelming sense of terror and dismay, a wrenching sensation of sinfulness and guilt. When God spoke, Abram stretched himself upon the ground to listen. When Moses saw the Lord in the burning bush, he hid his face in fear to look upon God. Isaiah's vision of God wrung from him the cry, "Woe is me!" and the confession, "I am undone; because I am a man of unclean lips."

These experiences show that a vision of the divine transcendence soon ends all controversy between the man and his God. The fight goes out of the man and he is ready with the conquered Saul to ask meekly, "Lord, what wilt thou have me to do?"

—A. W. Tozer

The fear of God kills all other fears.

—Hugh Black

> **CHARACTER CHECK**
>
> Sometime soon, go to your favorite, quietest, holiest place. And spend enough time there till you feel God's presence over you, around you, behind you. He's awesome, isn't He?

Jeremiah
Obedience to His Calling

from Jeremiah 20

There were days when Jeremiah would have given anything to be someone else because this call was costing him everything. His friends. His reputation. Perhaps even his life, if some people had their way. But the fire he feared most was the one that burned inside of him.

Look at It This Way

Jeremiah's main beef was with the religious and political establishment of his day, those priests and rulers who shouldered the responsibility for serving God's people and inspiring them to holiness. In their greed and grasp for power—and in the grip of their own bondage to sin—they had lost the credibility and discernment to lead as God desired.

"They dress the wound of my people as though it were not serious," Jeremiah would say. And still today, when immorality and pride masquerades as authority, the wounds go untreated. Sin escalates. Pain perseveres.

First, a Quick Read

O Lord, you deceived me, and I was deceived;
    you overpowered me and prevailed.
I am ridiculed all day long;
    everyone mocks me.
Whenever I speak, I cry out
    proclaiming violence and destruction.
So the word of the Lord has brought me
    insult and reproach all day long.
But if I say, "I will not mention him
    or speak any more in his name,"
his word is in my heart like a fire,
    a fire shut up in my bones.
I am weary of holding it in;
    indeed, I cannot.
I hear many whispering,
    "Terror on every side!
    Report him! Let's report him!"
All my friends are waiting for me to slip, saying,
    "Perhaps he will be deceived;
    then we will prevail over him
    and take our revenge on him."

> But the LORD is with me like a mighty warrior;
>> so my persecutors will stumble and not prevail.
> They will fail and be thoroughly disgraced;
>> their dishonor will never be forgotten.
> O LORD Almighty, you who examine the righteous
>> and probe the heart and mind,
> let me see your vengeance upon them,
>> for to you I have committed my cause.
>
> Jeremiah 20:7–12

When You Think about It

We do all as unto the Lord and not unto other people. We live with our Lord in view. We look always to the "author and finisher of our faith" (Heb. 12:1–2). When our focus is on people and whether they follow us, respond favorably to us, affirm us, or recognize us with gifts and praise, we are courting pain and disappointment. Our peace in ministry comes from a strong and clear relationship with God. He gives the affirmation; He provides His love—and this is enough!

God's wonderful provision for life at God's best is a life lived in, controlled by, and responsive to the Holy Spirit's presence and power. What we cannot do, He can and will do. No one can make me angry when the Holy Spirit is controlling me. Nothing can disturb the peace of God in me when He is in control of me.

Deliberately cultivating the life of the Son of God in me is crucial to peace and contentment in my life and ministry. When my life is lived with His peace, then I can lead others to experience His peace as well.

—Henry Blackaby

> **CHARACTER CHECK**
>
> Expect some major-league challenges to the calling God has placed on your life. And when you feel like quitting, take it as a warning that you're trying to do it all yourself.

Only he who keeps his eye fixed on the far horizon will find his right road.

—Dag Hammarskjold

Shadrach, Meshach, and Abednego
No Compromise

from Daniel 3

Imagine being in a sold-out stadium with thousands of ravenous hometown fans, and you're the only one wearing the opponents' colors. That was the situation for these three Hebrew boys. But nothing was going to keep them from standing up for their side.

First, a Quick Read

King Nebuchadnezzar made an image of gold, ninety feet high and nine feet wide, and set it up on the plain of Dura in the province of Babylon. . . .

At this time some astrologers came forward and denounced the Jews. They said to King Nebuchadnezzar, "O king, live for ever! You have issued a decree, O king, that everyone who hears the sound of the horn, flute, zither, lyre, harp, pipes and all kinds of music must fall down and worship the image of gold, and that whoever does not fall down and worship will be thrown into a blazing furnace. But there are some Jews whom you have set over the affairs of the province of Babylon—Shadrach, Meshach and Abednego—who pay no attention to you, O king. They neither serve your gods nor worship the image of gold you have set up."

Shadrach, Meshach and Abednego replied to the king, . . . "If we are thrown into the blazing furnace, the God we serve is able to save us from it, and he will rescue us from your hand, O king. But even if he does not, we want you to know, O king, that we will not serve your gods or worship the image of gold you have set up."

Daniel 3:1, 8–12, 16a, 17–18

LOOK AT IT THIS WAY

Shadrach, Meshach, and Abednego were part of a select group of young Hebrew boys who were deported from their homeland and conscripted as leadership trainees in the courts of Babylon. It was a practice that stripped Israel of her brightest and best, but it couldn't strip away the godly heritage of those who had been raised to worship the one true God.

Our children face a world with ample opportunities for compromise. By building a base of truth and Christian character beneath them, you can strengthen their inclination for sound, moral choices.

When You Think about It

A somewhat common practice in the business world is to consider people who take a stand for issues of conscience as suspect, threatening, or even perhaps as losers who should be passed over by others who are more willing to play the game. I truly believe that taking a stand for issues of character, honesty, and fair practice will, in the long run, cause one to prosper in all the right ways. However, if one is going to be a man or woman of integrity, one needs to realize that it may, in the short run, be very costly.

I know people who have gone through difficult situations and are bitter at God for not rescuing them from their own fiery furnaces. They feel as though the Lord abandoned them. They feel justified in their moral lapses because God didn't come through for them as they thought He should.

These three young friends of Daniel's were committed to do what was right without respect to the outcome—whether it benefited them or cost them everything. They so greatly valued their integrity, they were willing to pay the ultimate price to stand for what was right.

—Jim Henry

An absolute standard cannot be compromised. It can only be broken.

—Richard Niebuhr

> **CHARACTER CHECK**
>
> The pressure to conform is a condition you never outgrow. But with practice, you can build enough biblical boundaries around yourself to stand up to the most compromising situations.

Daniel
Faithfulness without Reward

from Daniel 5

Think, Belshazzar! Put yourself in Daniel's shoes. If you were the wise man, bearing critical information of interest to the crown, what would you want in return? Riches? Yes, and recognition. Maybe a new title for your business card. Daniel says no? What is it this guy *wants*?

Look at It This Way

Daniel had been in this spot before, as a junior member of Nebuchadnezzar's mystical advisory board. When the king had ordered an ax to every one of their necks for failing to interpret his dream, Daniel was the only one with a true God to consult and the only one brave enough to give the king a less-than-pleasant report.

Spiritual growth builds on spiritual experience. And like Daniel, our confidence in following the Lord's nudgings will grow as we get used to the sound of His voice.

First, a Quick Read

King Belshazzar gave a great banquet for a thousand of his nobles and drank wine with them. . . .

Suddenly the fingers of a human hand appeared and wrote on the plaster of the wall, near the lampstand in the royal palace. The king watched the hand as it wrote. . . .

So Daniel was brought before the king, and the king said to him, "Are you Daniel, one of the exiles my father the king brought from Judah? I have heard that the spirit of the gods is in you and that you have insight, intelligence and outstanding wisdom. The wise men and enchanters were brought before me to read this writing and tell me what it means, but they could not explain it. Now I have heard that you are able to give interpretations and to solve difficult problems. If you can read this writing and tell me what it means, you will be clothed in purple and have a gold chain placed around your neck, and you will be made the third highest ruler in the kingdom."

Then Daniel answered the king, "You may keep your gifts for yourself and give your rewards to someone else. Nevertheless, I will read the writing for the king and tell him what it means."

Daniel 5:1, 5, 13–17

When You Think about It

Faithfulness is consecration in overalls. It is the steady acceptance and performance of the common duty and the immediate task without any reference to personal preferences—because it is there to be done and so is a manifestation of the will of God.

Faithfulness means continuing quietly with the job we have been given, in the situation where we have been placed, not yielding to the restless desire for change. It means tending the lamp quietly for God without wondering how much longer it has got to go on. Steady, unsensational driving, taking good care of the car. It means keeping everything in your charge in good order for love's sake, rubbing up the silver, polishing the glass even though you know the Master will not be looking"—round the pantry next weekend. If your life is really part of the apparatus of the Spirit, that is the sort of life it must be. You have got to be the sort of cat who can be left alone with the canary: the sort of dog who follows, hungry and thirsty but tail up, to the very end of the day.
—Evelyn Underhill

What is the ruling principle of your life? Is it the love of God? Is it the fear of God? Or is it neither of these, but rather the love of the world.
—John Wesley

CHARACTER CHECK

Would you work harder for more pay? More responsibility? A company car? If perks don't turn your head, then you can be pretty sure you're working for the right reasons.

Jonah
Running from God
from Jonah 1

Street preaching has never been an easy job, and anyone who is called to it must come equipped with a thick-skinned hide for unholy accusations and feet that are able to stand toe-to-toe with the nastiest dissenters. But when Jonah got the call, his feet weren't in it.

First, a Quick Read

The word of the LORD came to Jonah son of Amittai: "Go to the great city of Nineveh and preach against it, because its wickedness has come up before me."

But Jonah ran away from the LORD and headed for Tarshish. He went down to Joppa, where he found a ship bound for that port. After paying the fare, he went aboard and sailed for Tarshish to flee from the LORD.

Then the LORD sent a great wind on the sea, and such a violent storm arose that the ship threatened to break up. . . .

This terrified them and they asked, "What have you done?" (They knew he was running away from the LORD, because he had already told them so.) The sea was getting rougher and rougher. So they asked him, "What should we do to you to make the sea calm down for us?"

"Pick me up and throw me into the sea," he replied, "and it will become calm. I know that it is my fault that this great storm has come upon you." . . .

Then they took Jonah and threw him overboard, and the raging sea grew calm. . . .

But the LORD provided a great fish to swallow Jonah, and Jonah

---

LOOK AT IT THIS WAY

Jonah ran into some stiff headwinds during his flight from God's orders. That's because God's mercy and love don't always dress in their nicest clothes.

Sometimes God loves us as he did Jonah—with hardship. He knows that His plans hold our only hope for joy and fulfillment. He further knows that when our own plans dwindle into disarray, we will turn to Him with a passion we might never have known had it not been for His love showing up in a less than a favorable light—and making everything make sense again.

was inside the fish three days and three nights.

Jonah 1:1–4, 10–12, 15, 17

When You Think about It

After you give yourself to the Lord, He begins to break what is offered to Him. Everything seems to go wrong, and you protest and find fault with the ways of God. But to stay there is to be no more than just a broken vessel—no good for the world, because you have gone too far for the world to use you, and no good for God either, because you have not gone far enough for Him to use you. You are out of gear with the world, and you have a controversy with God. This is the tragedy of many a Christian.

My giving of myself to the Lord must be an initial fundamental act. Then, day by day, I must go on giving to him, not finding fault with his use of me, but accepting with praise even what the flesh finds hard.

I am the Lord's, and now no longer reckon myself to be my own, but acknowledge in everything His ownership and authority. That is the attitude God delights in, and to maintain it is true consecration. May we always be possessed by the consciousness that we are not our own.

—Watchman Nee

The Lord cannot fully bless a man until he has first conquered him.

—A. W. Tozer

> **CHARACTER CHECK**
>
> Your struggle probably is not with running from God but with knowing exactly where He's wanting you. Keep praying. Keep listening. And do faithfully the things you *do* know.

Habakkuk
Trusting God Anyway

from Habakkuk 1 & 3

Judah was enjoying the glorious fruit of Josiah's social reforms. Meanwhile, Assyria, once the scourge of the Middle East, was only a shadow of its former self. But now, muddying the carpet of peace and promise, were the barbarous Babylonians. "How long, O Lord?"

Look at It This Way

Your boss may think you're a nut for believing in God. Trust God anyway. Your spouse may think you carry your faith a little too far. Trust God anyway. Your family may think you're cushioning yourself and your children from the real world. Trust God anyway.

Your health may be failing. Trust God anyway. Your stress may be unbearable. Trust God anyway. Your career track may seem like it's on a slow train to nowhere. Trust God anyway.

To make it in this Christian life, there's only one way. And it's to trust God. Anyway.

First, a Quick Read

How long, O LORD, must I call for help,
    but you do not listen?
Or cry out to you, "Violence!"
    but you do not save?
Why do you make me look at injustice?
    Why do you tolerate wrong?
Destruction and violence are before me;
    there is strife, and conflict abounds.
Therefore the law is paralyzed,
    and justice never prevails.
The wicked hem in the righteous,
    so that justice is perverted. . . .
LORD, I have heard of your fame;
    I stand in awe of your deeds, O LORD.
Renew them in our day,
    in our time make them known;
    in wrath remember mercy. . . .
Yet I will wait patiently for the day of calamity
    to come on the nation invading us.
Though the fig tree does not bud
    and there are no grapes on the vines,

though the olive crop fails
>and the fields produce no food,
though there are no sheep in the pen
>and no cattle in the stalls,
yet I will rejoice in the LORD,
>I will be joyful in God my Savior.
The Sovereign LORD is my strength;
>he makes my feet like the feet of a deer,
>he enables me to go on the heights.

>>Habakkuk 1:2–4; 3:2, 16b–19

When You Think about It

Habakkuk 2:4 describes the person who can survive such testing times. "See, he is puffed up; his desires are not upright—but the righteous will live by his faith." The person in the right relation to God and to his fellows will live by simply being faithful. That is, people will live by faithfully doing every day what in faith they were accustomed to doing. The formula for survival in hard times is faithful humility—standing under the load, as the New Testament puts it. That is why the righteous outlive the tyrants.

The Book of Habakkuk represents the kind of faith that became the norm for Judaism and later for Christianity. Israel no longer had the means to try to shape their own destiny. Under the empires, they were the passive recipients of whatever good or evil the powerful chose to give them. But in faith they could believe that God, through those whom He allowed to rule, would provide what was necessary for His people to serve God. Believing and waiting became essential elements in their way of life. It should still be so.

>—*Holman Bible Handbook*

CHARACTER CHECK

Make up your mind that nothing will ever make you doubt the reality of God, the hope of His eternal kingdom, and the promise that He is working all things for your good.

Look within and be depressed. Look without and be distressed. Look at Jesus and be at rest.

>—Corrie ten Boom

ZECHARIAH
Questioning God

from Luke 1

Zechariah was an old man. His idea of excitement was watching an auburn sunset bathe the Judean hillsides in fiery light or swapping stories with his friends around the temple. Won't he be dumbfounded to find out—at *his* age—that he's going to be a first-time daddy?

LOOK AT IT THIS WAY

"Your prayer has been heard." Prayer? What prayer? Oh, Zechariah had prayed numerous times back when Elizabeth was of childbearing age. For forty years or more he had prayed. But after a while, you just resign yourself to the facts.

Wonder how long God had been saving that prayer—like a letter folded up in his breast pocket, waiting for just the right time to answer it? If he'd answered it any sooner, no one would have paid attention. *So Elizabeth is expecting? Well, it's about time.* But this way, it was about God.

First, a Quick Read

Once when Zechariah's division was on duty and he was serving as priest before God, an angel of the Lord appeared to him, standing at the right side of the altar of incense. When Zechariah saw him, he was startled and was gripped with fear. But the angel said to him: "Do not be afraid, Zechariah; your prayer has been heard. Your wife Elizabeth will bear you a son, and you are to give him the name John." . . .

Zechariah asked the angel, "How can I be sure of this? I am an old man and my wife is well along in years."

The angel answered, . . . "You will be silent and not able to speak until the day this happens, because you did not believe my words, which will come true at their proper time." . . .

When it was time for Elizabeth to have her baby, she gave birth to a son. . . .

On the eighth day they came to circumcise the child, and they were going to name him after his father Zechariah. . . .

Then they made signs to his father, to find out what he would like to name the child. He asked for a writing tablet, and to everyone's astonishment he wrote, "His name is John."

Luke 1:8, 11–13, 18–19a, 20, 57, 59, 62–63

When You Think about It

Doubt is not the opposite of faith but an element of faith. I have faith that there is an all-loving God in spite of the fact that I have no sure way of knowing that there is.

In short, we look at the world and conclude from what we find that, all evidence to the contrary notwithstanding, we will, like Pascal, place our wager on God. Our faith is that wager.

We can take great heart from Saint Paul's words to the Corinthians that although now we see only through a glass darkly, there will come a day when we will see face to face and understand even as we are fully understood. It is the nature of faith to look beyond itself—and beyond the doubts that must always exist in tension with it, if it is a living faith—to a time on the far side of time when the holy dream is at last revealed to be reality, and all that we take now for reality glimmers like a dream. In the meanwhile, faith is the way we have of seeing while we have only the dark glass to see through.

—Frederick Buechner

What grounds do you have for not believing God?
—D. L. Moody

CHARACTER CHECK

When God's Word asks you to believe something that's simply beyond belief, then you get to decide: Will you trust your five senses or have sense enough to believe Him?

Joseph: Staying in God's Will

from Matthew 1

He knew that he hadn't—he hoped and prayed that she hadn't—this just couldn't be happening. Still, Mary had never been known to lie to him before. What's a nice guy like Joseph doing in a mess like this? To help us see the miracles that occur inside of God's will.

Look at It This Way

Does God ever speak to you in dreams? The Bible certainly bears out the practice. Joseph, Jacob, Nebuchadnezzar, and others. Job's friend, Elihu, said: "For God does speak" now one way, now another— / though man may not perceive it. / In a dream, in a vision of the night, / when deep sleep falls on men as they slumber in their beds" (Job 33:14–15).

Certainly dreams are often born from the day's events or from pizza eaten too late at night. But stay open to God's communicating through your dreams. It's been done before.

First, a Quick Read

This is how the birth of Jesus Christ came about: His mother Mary was pledged to be married to Joseph, but before they came together, she was found to be with child through the Holy Spirit.

Because Joseph her husband was a righteous man and did not want to expose her to public disgrace, he had in mind to divorce her quietly.

But after he had considered this, an angel of the Lord appeared to him in a dream and said, "Joseph son of David, do not be afraid to take Mary home as your wife, because what is conceived in her is from the Holy Spirit. She will give birth to a son, and you are to give him the name Jesus, because he will save his people from their sins."

All this took place to fulfill what the Lord had said through the prophet: "The virgin will be with child and will give birth to a son, and they will call him Immanuel"—which means, "God with us."

When Joseph woke up, he did what the angel of the Lord had commanded him and took Mary home as his wife. But he had no union with her until she gave birth to a son. And he gave him the name Jesus.

Matthew 1:18–25

When You Think about It

Many of us want God to speak to us and give us an assignment. However, we are not interested in making any major adjustments in our lives. Biblically, that is impossible. Every time God spoke to people in Scripture about something He wanted to do through them, major adjustments were necessary. They had to adjust their lives to God. Once the adjustments were made, God accomplished His purposes through those He called.

Adjustments may be required in one or more of the following areas: In your circumstances (like job, home, finances). In your relationships (family, friends, business associates). In your thinking (prejudices, methods, your potential). In your commitments (to family, church, job, plans, tradition). In your actions (how you pray, give, serve). In your beliefs (about God, His purposes, His ways, your relationship to Him). The list could go on an on.

To go from your ways, thoughts, and purposes to God's will always requires a major adjustment. Once you have made the necessary adjustments, you can follow God in obedience. Keep in mind—the God who calls you is also the One who will enable you to do His will.

—Henry Blackaby

To know the will of God is the greatest knowledge. To do the will of God is the greatest achievement.

—George W. Truett

> **CHARACTER CHECK**
>
> God's work is bigger than any one person yet is performed through a God-guided network of individuals who are willing to swim the currents of His will. Are you?

Simeon
Never Stop Waiting

from Luke 2

Most of us would have given up on God years before. But you get the feeling that Simeon never lost hope in God's promise. If he was to see the Messiah in his lifetime, then God was just going to have to extend his lifetime. And Simeon would be there waiting.

LOOK AT IT THIS WAY

Waiting requires trust. To stand on a rainy sidewalk waiting for your wife to pick you up after work is to trust that she'll be there as soon as she can. To wait for the start of football season is to trust that, come September, your favorite team will be teeing it up.

For Simeon, waiting didn't mean he knew exactly what he was waiting for. There were no three-simple-steps for spotting the Messiah. His motivation for waiting was based on one thing alone. He trusted God. And that made it worth the wait.

First, a Quick Read

When the time of their purification according to the Law of Moses had been completed, Joseph and Mary took him to Jerusalem to present him to the Lord (as it is written in the Law of the Lord, "Every firstborn male is to be consecrated to the Lord"), and to offer a sacrifice in keeping with what is said in the Law of the Lord: "a pair of doves or two young pigeons."

Now there was a man in Jerusalem called Simeon, who was righteous and devout. He was waiting for the consolation of Israel, and the Holy Spirit was upon him. It had been revealed to him by the Holy Spirit that he would not die before he had seen the Lord's Christ. Moved by the Spirit, he went into the temple courts. When the parents brought in the child Jesus to do for him what the custom of the Law required, Simeon took him in his arms and praised God, saying:

"Sovereign Lord, as you have promised,
 you now dismiss your servant in peace.
For my eyes have seen your salvation,
 which you have prepared in the sight of all people,
a light for revelation to the Gentiles
 and for glory to your people Israel."

Luke 2:22–32

When You Think about It

The Lord graciously laid me aside once in my life for a number of months and put me, spiritually, into utter darkness. It was almost as though he had forsaken me, almost as though nothing was going on and I had really come to the end of everything. And then by degrees, he brought things back again.

We cannot face the thought that God will keep us aside for so long a time; we cannot bear to wait. And of course, I cannot tell you how long he will take. It will seem as though nothing is happening; as though everything you valued is slipping from your grasp. There confronts you a blank wall with no door in it. Seemingly, everyone is being blessed and used, while you yourself have been passed by and are losing out.

Lie quiet. All is in darkness, but it is only for a night. It must indeed be a full night, but that is all. Afterwards, you will find that everything is given back to you in glorious resurrection; and nothing can measure the difference between what was before and what now is!

—Watchman Nee

One doesn't discover new lands without consenting to lose sight of the shore for a very long time.

—André Gide

CHARACTER CHECK

Waiting doesn't come with instructions, shortcuts, and high adventure. But what it lacks in fun, it makes up for in fulfillment. God's blessings come to those who wait in faith.

John the Baptist
Accepting a Supporting Role

from John 1

Less understanding philosophers might look at the story of John the Baptist and say life was cruel to him, that he was forced to cross a fatal line in history that short-circuited his effectiveness and ruined his search for personal meaning and purpose. What do they know?

Look at It This Way

Let's look at this a different way. We're used to the sermon about not seeking the spotlight. So even when we're tempted to want a taste of the glory, we're usually smart enough to hide it.

But consider the possibility that God may want you to be more visible. He may have good reason for your work to be recognized, or your testimony to be shared. "God has arranged the parts in the body, every one of them, just as he wanted them to be" (1 Cor. 12:18). Would you say no if He wanted you noticed?

First, a Quick Read

Now this was John's testimony when the Jews of Jerusalem sent priests and Levites to ask him who he was. He did not fail to confess, but confessed freely, "I am not the Christ." . . .

Finally they said, "Who are you? Give us an answer to take back to those who sent us. What do you say about yourself?"

John replied in the words of Isaiah the prophet, "I am the voice of one calling in the desert, 'Make straight the way for the Lord.'"

Now some Pharisees who had been sent questioned him, "Why then do you baptize if you are not the Christ, nor Elijah, nor the Prophet?"

"I baptize with water," John replied, "but among you stands one you do not know." . . .

The next day John saw Jesus coming toward him and said, "Look, the Lamb of God, who takes away the sin of the world! This is the one I meant when I said, 'A man who comes after me has surpassed me because he was before me.' I myself did not know him, but the reason I came baptizing with water was that he might be revealed to Israel."

John 1:19–20, 22–26, 29–31

When You Think about It

The purpose of the best man is simply to stand with the groom, to make sure all attention is riveted on him. The best man would be a fool if in the middle of the wedding processional, he suddenly turned to the wedding guests and began to sing a song or engage in a humorous monologue. The best man has fulfilled his purpose most admirably when he draws no attention to himself, but focuses all attention upon the bride and groom.

And that is what John did. If Jesus Christ was the groom, then the Baptizer was committed to being the best man *and nothing else*. That was the purpose that flowed from his call, and he had no desire to anything beyond. Thus to see the crowd headed toward Christ was all the affirmation John needed; his purpose had been fulfilled.

"He must increase, but I must decrease," he said to those who had queried him about his attitude. What John had started out to accomplish—the introduction of Christ as the Lamb of God—had been accomplished. Having made the connection, John was satisfied and ready to withdraw.
—Gordon MacDonald

It is not what we do that matters, but what a Sovereign God chooses to do through us.
—Chuck Colson

CHARACTER CHECK

The truly Christian attitude is to neither be seeking the spotlight nor seeking the corner, but to be seeking the place God desires for you. And giving Him thanks wherever that is.

The Centurion
Submitting to God's Authority

from Matthew 8

The doctors had done all they could. The prognosis was hopeless. His servant was dying. So the centurion's options had been whittled down to two. Cry out to Caesar and the Roman gods. Or do something that seemed to have a better chance of working—*find this Jesus!*

Look at It This Way

By connecting his observations on authority with their greater realities in the spiritual world, the centurion revealed a powerful tool in the workshop of Christian understanding: There is nothing that exists around us that doesn't have a deeper, more eternal meaning.

Seeds becoming trees paint a picture of life after death. Geese flying in formation reflect an image of God's order. Even smelly garbage can teach a lesson about sin's nasty results. The things we see around us are much more than scenery. They're lenses for looking more closely at life.

First, a Quick Read

When Jesus had entered Capernaum, a centurion came to him, asking for help. "Lord," he said, "my servant lies at home paralyzed and in terrible suffering."

Jesus said to him, "I will go and heal him."

The centurion replied, "Lord, I do not deserve to have you come under my roof. But just say the word, and my servant will be healed. For I myself am a man under authority, with soldiers under me. I tell this one, 'Go,' and he goes; and that one, 'Come,' and he comes. I say to my servant, 'Do this,' and he does it."

When Jesus heard this, he was astonished and said to those following him, "I tell you the truth, I have not found anyone in Israel with such great faith. I say to you that many will come from the east and the west, and will take their places at the feast with Abraham, Isaac and Jacob in the kingdom of heaven. But the subjects of the kingdom will be thrown outside, into the darkness, where there will be weeping and gnashing of teeth."

Then Jesus said to the centurion, "Go! It will be done just as you believed it would." And his servant was healed at that very hour.

Matthew 8:5–13

When You Think about It

Do not be scared by the word *authority*. Believing things on authority only means believing them because you have been told them by someone you think trustworthy.

Ninety-nine percent of the things you believe are believed on authority. I believe there is such a place as New York. I have not seen it myself. I could not prove by abstract reasoning that there must be such a place. I believe it because reliable people have told me so. The ordinary man believes in the solar system, atoms, evolution, and the circulation of the blood on authority—because the scientists say so. Every historical statement in the world is believed on authority. None of us has seen the Norman Conquest or the defeat of the Armada. None of us could prove them by logic as you prove a thing in mathematics. We believe them simply because people who did see them have left writings that tell us about them: in fact, on authority.

A man who jibbed at authority in other things as some people do in religion would have to be content to know nothing all his life.
—C. S. Lewis

Because God is who He is and has such an impeccable character, we may be utterly sure our confidence in Him, our faith in Him, will never be betrayed.
—W. Phillip Keller

> **CHARACTER CHECK**
>
> God is in charge of this thing. And we can rest in the fact that His authority overrules sin, defeat, and hopelessness. Let Him reign on the throne of your life.

Bartimaeus
Believing in Miracles
from Mark 10 & Luke 11

He was making a scene, the kind that draws a stare, the kind that makes mothers grab their children by the hand and pull them close to their side. But the touch of God's hand was worth the risk of embarassment. At least, that's the way blind Bartimaeus saw it.

LOOK AT IT THIS WAY

You never know how you'll react in an emergency—to the blare of the siren, the whisk of the stretcher, the surprise of the late-night phone call. In moments of desperation, when you have nowhere else to turn, your reactions can run anywhere from panic to passive disbelief.

But if God has been your source of refuge for even the minor scrapes of life, if He's been your first resort during the tiniest tremors of life, then the big blows will only drive you where you've been all along—back on your knees.

First, a Quick Read

As Jesus and his disciples, together with a large crowd, were leaving the city, a blind man, Bartimaeus (that is, the Son of Timaeus), was sitting by the roadside begging. When he heard that it was Jesus of Nazareth, he began to shout, "Jesus, Son of David, have mercy on me!"

Many rebuked him and told him to be quiet, but he shouted all the more, "Son of David, have mercy on me!"

Jesus stopped and said, "Call him."

So they called to the blind man, "Cheer up! On your feet! He's calling you." Throwing his cloak aside, he jumped to his feet and came to Jesus.

"What do you want me to do for you?" Jesus asked him.

The blind man said, "Rabbi, I want to see."

"Go," said Jesus, "your faith has healed you."

Mark 10:46b–52a

Then he said to them, "Suppose one of you has a friend, and he goes to him at midnight and says, 'Friend, lend me three loaves of bread, because a friend of mine on a journey has come to me, and I have nothing to set before him.' . . .

"I tell you, though he will not get up and give him the bread because he is his friend, yet because of the man's boldness he will get up and give him as much as he needs."

Luke 11:5–6, 8

When You Think about It

The cry had reached the ear of the Lord. He knew what the man wanted and was ready to grant it to him. But before He did it, He asked him, "What wilt thou that I should do to thee?" He wanted to hear not only the general petition for mercy, but the distinct expression of what the man's desire was that day. Until he verbalized it, he was not healed.

There are still petitioners to whom the Lord puts the same question who cannot get the aid they need until they answer that question. Our prayers must be a distinct expression of definite need, not a vague appeal to His mercy or an indefinite cry for blessing. It isn't that His loving heart does not understand or is not ready to hear our cry. Rather, Jesus desires such definite prayer for our own sakes because it teaches us to know our own needs better. Time, thought, and self-scrutiny are required to find out what our greatest need really is. Our desires are put to the test to see whether they are honest and real and are according to God's Word.

—Andrew Murray

Jesus Christ is a God whom we approach without pride and before whom we humble ourselves without despair.

—Blaise Pascal

> **CHARACTER CHECK**
>
> Your brain may tell you differently, your friends may tell you differently, but when you honestly and truly believe God for the impossible, anything can happen.

Zacchaeus
Repaying for His Sins
from Luke 19

Little did the people of Jericho know that things were starting to look up the day Jesus caught sight of Zacchaeus in a sycamore tree. The wee little man with the grinch's heart was about to get a closer look at Jesus than he bargained for. Pass the tax refunds.

Look at It This Way

Restitution was an important biblical concept long before Zacchaeus inked his fingerprints on the pages of the New Testament. The Old Testament law required offenders to follow a two-step approach—restoring the value of the misused item or property to the rightful owner, as well as presenting a trespass offering to God on the altar. The message is clear. Guilt is never enough to right a wrong, and bitterness can leave behind a nasty build-up that hardens over the years. Is it pay-back time?

First, a Quick Read

Jesus entered Jericho and was passing through. A man was there by the name of Zacchaeus; he was a chief tax collector and was wealthy. He wanted to see who Jesus was, but being a short man he could not, because of the crowd. So he ran ahead and climbed a sycamore-fig tree to see him, since Jesus was coming that way.

When Jesus reached the spot, he looked up and said to him, "Zacchaeus, come down immediately. I must stay at your house today." So he came down at once and welcomed him gladly.

All the people saw this and began to mutter, "He has gone to be the guest of a 'sinner.'"

But Zacchaeus stood up and said to the Lord, "Look, Lord! Here and now I give half of my possessions to the poor, and if I have cheated anybody out of anything, I will pay back four times the amount."

Jesus said to him, "Today salvation has come to this house, because this man, too, is a son of Abraham. For the Son of Man came to seek and to save what was lost."

Luke 19:1–10

When You Think about It

There are some people who do not believe in sudden conversions. I should like them to tell me when Zacchaeus was converted. He certainly was not converted when he went *up into* the sycamore tree; he certainly was converted when he came down. He must have been converted somewhere between the branches and the ground.

I wish we had a few men converted like Zacchaeus here in London; it would make no small stir. When a man begins to make restitution, it is a pretty good sign of conversion. Zacchaeus gave half his goods all at once, and he said, "If I have taken anything from any man, I restore him fourfold." I imagine the next morning, one of the servants of Zacchaeus going with a check for $1,000, and saying, "A few years ago, my master took from you wrongfully about $250, and this is restitution money." That would give confidence in Zacchaeus's conversion.

Unless our repentance includes conversion, it is not worth much. It's like pumping away continually at the ship's pumps without stopping the leaks. Prayer and confession would be of no avail while they continued in sin.
—D. L. Moody

We cannot continue to enjoy the fruits of the sins we want to be forgiven.
—John R. W. Stott

Character Check

Back tithes and unrestored relationships can choke your ability to receive the full freedom of forgiveness. Ask God to show you how to make good on your bad decisions.

Nicodemus
Converted out of His Culture
from John 3 & 19

Nicodemus knew his religion like the back of his hand. Ask him anything, and he'd at least give you an answer that sounded good. But this so-called Messiah was sort of horning in on his territory, loosening the boards of a belief platform that he had nailed down years ago.

LOOK AT IT THIS WAY

Many of us who shake our heads at our Sunday lawn-mowing neighbors while adjusting our neckties in the living room mirror need to check ourselves a little closer. Are we truly going to church to worship God? Or is that simply our culture of choice—like a patio breakfast with the Sunday paper is to the folks next door?

Let's never get so caught up in our church culture—like the Pharisees in Nicodemus's day—that we miss the higher purpose of our faith. That's what our neighbors are really wanting to see.

First, a Quick Read

Now there was a man of the Pharisees named Nicodemus, a member of the Jewish ruling council. He came to Jesus at night and said, "Rabbi, we know you are a teacher who has come from God. For no one could perform the miraculous signs you are doing if God were not with him."

In reply Jesus declared, "I tell you the truth, no one can see the kingdom of God unless he is born again."

"How can a man be born when he is old?" Nicodemus asked. "Surely he cannot enter a second time into his mother's womb to be born!" . . .

How can this be?" Nicodemus asked. . . .

"How . . . I have spoken to you of earthly things and you do not believe; how then will you believe if I speak of heavenly things?" . . .

Later, Joseph of Arimathea asked Pilate for the body of Jesus. Now Joseph was a disciple of Jesus, but secretly because he feared the Jews. With Pilate's permission, he came and took the body away. He was accompanied by Nicodemus, the man who earlier had visited Jesus at night. Nicodemus brought a mixture of myrrh and aloes, about seventy-five pounds.

John 3:1–4, 9, 12; 19:38–39

When You Think about It

You must picture me alone in that room in Magdalen, night after night, feeling, whenever my mind lifted even for a second from my work, the steady, unrelenting approach of Him whom I so earnestly desired not to meet. That which I greatly feared had at last come upon me. In the Trinity Term of 1929, I gave in, and admitted that God was God, and knelt and prayed: perhaps, that night, the most dejected and reluctant convert in all England. I did not then see what is now the most shining and obvious thing; the Divine humility which will accept a convert even on such terms. The Prodigal Son at least walked home on his own feet. But who can duly adore the Love which will open the high gates to a prodigal who is brought in kicking, struggling, resentful, and darting his eyes in every direction for a chance to escape? The words *compelle itrare*, compel them to come in, have been so abused; but, properly understood, they plumb the depth of the Divine mercy. The hardness of God is kinder than the softness of men, and His compulsion is our liberation.

—C. S. Lewis

Too late have I loved You, O Beauty so ancient and so new, too late have I loved You!

—Augustine

CHARACTER CHECK

There are unsaved people within your reach who are starting to see the holes in their habits. They're asking questions only God has the answer to. And you'd be a great person to tell them.

Thomas
Seeing Is Believing

from John 20 & 1 Peter 1

Thomas was a five-senses kind of guy trying to feel his way through a situation that made absolutely no sense. I mean, you just don't die one minute and then wake up seventy-two hours later as if nothing's happened. Who could believe a thing like that? Could you?

Look at It This Way

Carl Sagan once said he didn't want to believe. He wanted to know.

He follows in a long line of the unsure and unsatisfied who never understood that faith has a jumping-off place where the next step costs you the safety of your own assurances. It's not a trick implemented by a God who delights in watching people shiver on the high dive, but the far-sighted plan of a loving Father who longs for you to let Him hold you in His arms—and hear you ask if you can jump again.

First, a Quick Read

Now Thomas (called Didymus), one of the Twelve, was not with the disciples when Jesus came. So the other disciples told him, "We have seen the Lord!"

But he said to them, "Unless I see the nail marks in his hands and put my finger where the nails were, and put my hand into his side, I will not believe it."

A week later his disciples were in the house again, and Thomas was with them. Though the doors were locked, Jesus came and stood among them and said, "Peace be with you!" Then he said to Thomas, "Put your finger here; see my hands. Reach out your hand and put it into my side. Stop doubting and believe."

Thomas said to him, "My Lord and my God!"

Then Jesus told him, "Because you have seen me, you have believed; blessed are those who have not seen and yet have believed."

John 20:24–29

Though you have not seen him, you love him; and even though you do not see him now, you believe in him and are filled with an inexpressible and glorious joy, for you are receiving the goal of your faith, the salvation of your souls.

1 Peter 1:8–9

When You Think about It

Thomas should have believed on the basis of the evidence that he had from the other disciples and which was quite sufficient. Jesus said, "Because you have seen me, you have believed; blessed are those who have not seen and yet have believed." Is Jesus saying by this that believing is a blind leap of ungrounded faith? Quite the opposite! Because Thomas insisted on seeing and touching Jesus in His resurrected body, we have been given in the Gospels an even clearer evidence of the Resurrection than we would otherwise have had. But Jesus is saying that Thomas should have believed without this additional evidence, because the evidence available to Thomas before was in itself sufficient. In other words, before Thomas saw and heard Jesus in this way, he was in the same position as we are today. Both he at that time and we today have the same sufficient witness of those who have seen and heard and who have had the opportunity to touch the resurrected Christ. In fact, in the light of this sufficient and sure witness, we, like Thomas, are disobedient if we do not bow. We are without excuse.
—Francis Schaeffer

Faith in the unseen is what faith is all about.
—F. LaGard Smith

> **CHARACTER CHECK**
>
> Believing in Jesus is really an easy step, complicated only by the nervous pleadings of our own pride and fear. Take it from Thomas. He only wishes he'd have dived in sooner.

Joseph of Arimathea
Meeting Practical Needs

from Matthew 27; Luke 23; Romans 12

No one would have wanted Jesus' body to be tossed into a common grave with thieves and criminals. He'd been humiliated enough already. But everything had been so frightening, so sudden, so unbelievable. Nobody stopped to think about it. Well, almost nobody.

LOOK AT IT THIS WAY

There are so many little things we can do to show Christ's love to others—so little, in fact, we look right over their heads. But all it takes is a little thoughtfulness and a prayer for God's direction, and He can turn our smallest expressions into life-sized acts of ministry.

It'll cost us some time we used to spend concentrating on our own busy schedules, our own problems, our own concerns. But every minute we invest in trying to dream up new ways to serve God by serving others is time well spent.

First, a Quick Read

Jesus called out with a loud voice, "Father, into your hands I commit my spirit." When he had said this, he breathed his last. . . .

Now there was a man named Joseph, a member of the Council, a good and upright man, who had not consented to their decision and action. He came from the Judean town of Arimathea and he was waiting for the kingdom of God.

Luke 23:46, 50–51

Going to Pilate, he asked for Jesus' body, and Pilate ordered that it be given to him. Joseph took the body, wrapped it in a clean linen cloth, and placed it in his own new tomb that he had cut out of the rock. He rolled a big stone in front of the entrance to the tomb and went away.

Matthew 27:58–60

We have different gifts, according to the grace given us. If a man's gift is prophesying, let him use it in proportion to his faith. If it is serving, let him serve; if it is teaching, let him teach; if it is encouraging, let him encourage; if it is contributing to the needs of others, let him give generously; if it is leadership, let him govern diligently; if it is showing mercy, let him do it cheerfully.

Romans 12:6–8

When You Think about It

"Slave" is not a word most of us nowadays "feel comfortable" with. It is significant that most modern Bible translations use "servant" instead. For a slave is not his own, has no rights whatsoever, makes no choices about what he will do or how he is to serve.

Once we give up our slavery to the world, which is a cruel master indeed, to become Christ's bondslave, we live out our servitude to Him by glad service to others. This volunteer slavery cannot be taken advantage of—we have chosen to surrender everything for love. It is a wholly different thing from forced labor. It is, in fact, the purest joy when it is most unobserved, most un-self-conscious, most simple, most freely offered.

Lord, free me to be Your happy slave—that is, to be the happy foot-washer of anyone today who needs his feet washed, his supper cooked, his faults overlooked, his work commended, his failure forgiven, his griefs consoled, or his button sewed on. Let me not imagine that my love for You is very great if I am unwilling to do for a human being something very small.

—Elisabeth Elliot

We ought not to be weary of doing little things for the love of God, who regards not the greatness of the work, but the love with which it is performed.

—Brother Lawrence

CHARACTER CHECK

Make a point to save ten minutes this week just to think about some ways you can serve your family, your church, your friends in need. Do it practically anytime.

Peter Captured by Conscience

from Matthew 26; Luke 22; John 18

Peter honestly didn't see it coming. Looking back, he's not even sure it would have mattered. He was just weakened by the fear, by the confusion, by the snap in Christ's voice after Peter had taken a sharp-edged swipe at that arresting soldier. Could Jesus ever forgive him?

Look at It This Way

There is guilt. And then there is conviction. Guilt depresses, defeats, demoralizes. Conviction motivates and redirects. Guilt is a seed planted strategically by the devil that crops up at the most unexpected times to remind us how pathetic we are. Conviction is an uncommon gift from the Holy Spirit that may come wrapped in sandpaper and burn all the way down. But its purpose is to redeem, to restore, to renew. Embrace conviction—sandpaper and all. It's God's patient way of giving us another chance.

First, a Quick Read

Then Jesus told them, "This very night you will all fall away on account of me." . . .

Peter replied, "Even if all fall away on account of you, I never will."

"I tell you the truth," Jesus answered, "this very night, before the rooster crows, you will disown me three times."

Matthew 26:31a, 33–34

It was cold, and the servants and officials stood around a fire they had made to keep warm. Peter also was standing with them, warming himself.

John 18:18

A servant girl saw him seated there in the firelight. She looked closely at him and said, "This man was with him."

But he denied it. "Woman, I don't know him," he said.

A little later someone else saw him and said, "You also are one of them."

"Man, I am not!" Peter replied.

About an hour later another asserted, "Certainly this fellow was with him, for he is a Galilean."

Peter replied, "Man, I don't know what you're talking about!" Just as he was speaking, the rooster crowed.

The Lord turned and looked straight at Peter. Then Peter remembered the word the Lord had spoken to him.... And he went outside and wept bitterly.

Luke 22:56–61a, 62

When You Think about It

I think of Peter, who denied Jesus not once, but three times. How easy it would have been for Jesus to treat Peter bitterly, to make him feel as small as he had acted. But Jesus didn't say a word. Is that because Jesus understood how easy it is for us to betray even our best intentions when we're overwhelmed by insecurity and fear? Was that the brokenness Jesus saw in Peter?

Someone might suggest that surely there must have been cruelty in Jesus' eyes when "the Lord turned and looked straight at Peter." We all know those "looks that can kill." Had Jesus' glance been a look of cruelty, Peter might never have been salvaged. Instead, what Peter saw was a *knowing* look of *disappointment:* disappointment, because love hopes for the very best; knowing, because love recognizes human frailty.

Isn't that the way God works in our own lives? No one loves us more. And he loves us despite the fact that he knows us inside out. Instead of rebuking us cruelly, he gives us that—knowing look of disappointment,—and calls us higher.

—F. LaGard Smith

No instrument of torture can make a man so wretched as his own conscience when he is stretched upon its rack.

—Charles Spurgeon

> **CHARACTER CHECK**
>
> God knows how sick you are of that same old sin. He knows how badly you want to get beyond it. He knows it's more weakness than wickedness. And He's here to help you up.

PETER
Confident in Christ

from Matthew 16; Luke 9; Acts 2

You'd hardly believe this was the same fellow who couldn't even stand up for Christ to a young local girl around the campfire the night they sentenced his Master to death. Listen to him now—fearlessly firing off the hard facts. You haven't heard the last of this guy.

First, a Quick Read

Once when Jesus was praying in private and his disciples were with him, he asked them, "Who do the crowds say I am?"

They replied, "Some say John the Baptist; others say Elijah; and still others, that one of the prophets of long ago has come back to life."

Luke 9:18–19

"But what about you?" he asked. "Who do you say I am?"

Simon Peter answered, "You are the Christ, the Son of the living God."

Matthew 16:15–16

"Men of Israel, listen to this: Jesus of Nazareth was a man accredited by God to you by miracles, wonders and signs, which God did among you through him, as you yourselves know. This man was handed over to you by God's set purpose and foreknowledge; and you, with the help of wicked men, put him to death by nailing him to the cross. But God raised him from the dead, freeing him from the agony of death, because it was impossible for death to keep its hold on him. . . .

"Therefore let all Israel be assured of this: God has made this Jesus, whom you crucified, both Lord and Christ."

Acts 2:22–24, 36

LOOK AT IT THIS WAY

Charles Spurgeon said that few of us have an adequate idea of what we may become *even here on earth* by God's divine power and grace. We know one day we'll stand around the throne, with every pore in our being seeking a way to widen our praise. But if we just knew what He could do through us even now—with pride beat to a pulp, doubt driven out the back door, fear banished to the outfield. We can do everything through Him who gives us strength. Or were we just dreaming that?

When You Think about It

When God purposes to do something through you, the assignment will have God-sized dimensions. This is because God wants to reveal Himself to you and to those around you. If you can do the work in your own strength, people will not come to know God. However, if God works through you to do what only He can do, you and those around you will come to know Him. Jesus said, "He who does the truth comes to the light, that his deeds may be clearly seen, that they have been done in God" (John 3:21).

When other people see you experiencing God, they are going to want to know how they, too, can experience God that way. Be prepared to point them to God. You will need to be very careful that any testimony about what God has done only gives glory to Him. Pride may cause you to want to tell your experience because it makes you feel special. That will be a continuing tension. You must avoid any sense of pride. Therefore: "He who glories, let him glory in the Lord" (1 Cor. 1:31).

—Henry Blackaby

Our goal is not self-confidence. It is Christ-confidence.
—Charles Stanley

> **CHARACTER CHECK**
>
> If you're worried about the way your words will come out or concerned about the impression you'll leave behind, give God a chance to take over. You won't have a thing to worry about.

PETER Confronting Indiscretion

from Acts 5

One way of thinking says that Peter could have just let this whole thing go. After all, they did give a large offering to the church. How they arrived at the amount is their own business. But God's way of thinking said this was just the beginning. And He wanted it stopped.

LOOK AT IT THIS WAY

The Bible says there's more than one potential danger that can come from having to rebuke a brother. Besides the risk of appearing superior, besides the threat of someone's self-defense kicking in to make matters even more uncomfortable, there's always the possibility "you also may be tempted" (Gal. 6:1) to slacken your tolerance, to bend the Bible's teaching, to open your mind to the same kinds of seductions that have created the need for all this in the first place. "Watch yourself," the Word says. "Watch yourself."

First, a Quick Read

Now a man named Ananias, together with his wife Sapphira, also sold a piece of property. With his wife's full knowledge he kept back part of the money for himself, but brought the rest and put it at the apostles' feet.

Then Peter said, "Ananias, how is it that Satan has so filled your heart that you have lied to the Holy Spirit and have kept for yourself some of the money you received for the land? Didn't it belong to you before it was sold? And after it was sold, wasn't the money at your disposal? What made you think of doing such a thing? You have not lied to men but to God."

When Ananias heard this, he fell down and died. . . .

About three hours later his wife came in, not knowing what had happened. Peter asked her, "Tell me, is this the price you and Ananias got for the land?" "Yes," she said, "that is the price."

Peter said to her, "How could you agree to test the Spirit of the Lord? Look! The feet of the men who buried your husband are at the door, and they will carry you out also.". . .

Great fear seized the whole church and all who heard about these events.

Acts 5:1–5a, 7–9, 11

When You Think about It

When someone asked General Norman Schwarzkopf the secret of his success, he replied very simply, "I never walk past a problem." Another friend put it this way: "Just remember, when it comes to solving problems, the first price you pay is always the cheapest." We ignore problems, hoping they will go away, but that rarely happens. And the price of solving them goes up, not down.

Problems never get better when you ignore them. You may think you love someone too much to say anything. No, if you really loved him, you would speak the truth. You would speak it in love, but you would speak the truth he needed to hear. We are to love each other enough that we are willing for our brothers and sisters to hurt us if necessary.

Nobody wants to be hurt by his friends. We all want to be surrounded by people who will make us feel better about ourselves. But spiritual growth becomes possible when you let other people get close enough to you to say the things that you need to hear—whether you want to hear them or not.

—Ray Pritchard

A tolerance of sin that shuts its eyes to evil does great injustice, whether to children in the home or Christians in the church.

—Vance Havner

> **CHARACTER CHECK**
>
> Confrontations over issues of morality, money, and more are never easy, even when necessary. Pray long and hard about what God wants you to do. This is someone's life you're dealing with.

Peter Overcoming Prejudice

from Acts 10

Peter's repugnance at the sight of unclean food was an automatic, ingrained reflex. But his response to God's interpretation—that Peter needed to get used to the fact that the dreaded Gentiles were moving into the covenental neighborhood—was a sheer act of selfless surrender.

Look at It This Way

You may not consider yourself prejudiced at all. Racial reconciliation is so out in the open today, the blinders slip off fairly easily. But there's more than other colors that can cause you to see people in a different light. What about the rich? Or the educated? The movie bug, the union man, the sports talk junkie? Whenever we group individuals into neat classifications and judge them against our own likes and dislikes, we run the risk of letting our preconceptions drive the way we react. And isn't that what prejudice is, after all?

First, a Quick Read

Peter went up on the roof to pray. . . . He saw heaven opened and something like a large sheet being let down to earth by its four corners. It contained all kinds of four-footed animals, as well as reptiles of the earth and birds of the air.

Then a voice told him, "Get up, Peter. Kill and eat."

"Surely not, Lord!" Peter replied. "I have never eaten anything impure or unclean."

The voice spoke to him a second time, "Do not call anything impure that God has made clean." . . .

The following day he arrived in Caesarea. Cornelius was expecting them and had called together his relatives and close friends.

Talking with him, Peter went inside and found a large gathering of people. He said to them: "You are well aware that it is against our law for a Jew to associate with a Gentile or visit him. But God has shown me that I should not call any man impure or unclean. . . .

"I now realize how true it is that God does not show favoritism but accepts men from every nation who fear him and do what is right."

Acts 10:9b, 11–15, 24, 27–28, 34b–35

When You Think about It

The story is told of two people sitting across a table from one another. There is food on their plates, but the silverware is too long for them to get the food to their own mouth. For both to eat, they have to feed the other. The white community can feed the black community repentance and blessings. The black community can feed the white community forgiveness, acceptance, and unconditional love. Both have something that each needs.

God is impressing His church to reconcile itself to the hurtful pain and prejudice of the past and to live in the truth that we are one in Christ. I am often asked what the church has lost and what it hopes to find. I believe what has been lost is the model for living like Christ and, in turn, reaching out to others, looking for opportunities to be a servant.

We will continue to be trapped in the issues of race and color as long as we have a mind-set based on cultural differences. Jesus shows us that you do not reach a nation with culture; you reach a nation with character, the character of Christ.

—Wellington Boone

There is within every one of us a longing to do our part, to be one with God and one with each other.

—Phillip Porter

> **CHARACTER CHECK**
>
> Has something been telling you to open yourself to the possibility of your own prejudice? It's such a subtle sin, it's sometimes hard to spot. Pray for a way to make sure you're not infected.

Stephen
Paying the Ultimate Price

from Acts 6 & 7

Stephen knew that their looks could kill. And he had good reason to think their stones wouldn't be far behind. What makes a man able to look his own death squarely in the eye—to brace for the pain, to stand by the confession that seals his fate? Only God knows.

Look at It This Way

Stephen, though filled full of the Spirit, doesn't come off sounding like a natural-born troublemaker. He's not necessarily looking for a fight, just not willing to back down from one where his faith in Jesus is concerned.

You don't have to be a fearless firebrand to take a tough stand for Christ, only a faithful soldier who's willing to let God place you into situations that require the witness only you can give. The fire can get pretty hot, the looks can get pretty stony, but the Lord can keep you good and ready.

First, a Quick Read

Now Stephen, a man full of God's grace and power, did great wonders and miraculous signs among the people. Opposition arose, however, from members of the Synagogue of the Freedmen. . . .

So they stirred up the people and the elders and the teachers of the law. They seized Stephen and brought him before the Sanhedrin. . . .

"You stiff-necked people, with uncircumcised hearts and ears! You are just like your fathers: You always resist the Holy Spirit!" . . .

When they heard this, they were furious and gnashed their teeth at him. But Stephen, full of the Holy Spirit, looked up to heaven and saw the glory of God, and Jesus standing at the right hand of God. "Look," he said, "I see heaven open and the Son of Man standing at the right hand of God."

At this they covered their ears and, yelling at the top of their voices, they all rushed at him, dragged him out of the city and began to stone him. . . .

While they were stoning him, Stephen prayed, "Lord Jesus, receive my spirit." Then he fell on his knees and cried out, "Lord, do not hold this sin against them." When he had said this, he fell asleep.

Acts 6:8–9a, 12; 7:51, 54–58a, 59–60

When You Think about It

When you hear about Christians being martyred for their faith, do you think of biblical figures such as Stephen or John the Baptist? If you do, you're out of date by a couple thousand years. In fact, more Christians have been martyred for their faith in this century alone than in the previous nineteen centuries combined. More than followers of any other faith, Christians around the world are suffering brutal persecution. Volume upon volume of irrefutable, documented evidence continues to surface, revealing horrifying atrocities increasingly being committed against those who dare to follow Jesus Christ. The examples are heartbreakingly plentiful. The sheer dimensions of the problem are mind-boggling.

I wonder what God would do if all His people were on their knees begging for mercy for their persecuted brethren. Many things work against that kind of commitment. But with a crisis of this magnitude—blatant persecution—the consciences of Christians must be seared.

May God grant that Christians who are so comfortable in freedom never consider prayer too great an effort, stay informed, and speak out in defense of those who are willing to pay the ultimate price for their faith.
—Chuck Colson

Thousands that are capable of great sacrifices are yet not capable of the little ones which are all that are required of them.
—George MacDonald

> **CHARACTER CHECK**
>
> Whether you're in persecuted places of your own or wanting to help those who are, remember to pray. Remember to trust. Remember the martyrs.

Philip
Sensitive to the Spirit

from Acts 8

There's a language known only to the believer. Philip knew it. It's the language that resonates in a deep, hidden place about three buttons down your shirt and tells you something you have no logical way of knowing. It's the voice of the Spirit. Here's one who listened.

Look at It This Way

God cares about individuals. One of them works at the convenience market where you buy gas. You know him only as Matt. When you asked him why you hadn't seen him lately, he said he'd been to visit his grandfather, who's sick. You're sorry to hear that, you said. Is he better now? No, he said. They don't give him much time. A voice inside you says, Why not ask Matt what *he* would do if *he* knew *he* only had a few days to live. There's nobody behind you. You've got time. Stay sensitive.

First, a Quick Read

Those who had been scattered preached the word wherever they went. Philip went down to a city in Samaria and proclaimed the Christ there. When the crowds heard Philip and saw the miraculous signs he did, they all paid close attention to what he said. With shrieks, evil spirits came out of many, and many paralytics and cripples were healed. So there was great joy in that city. . . .

Now an angel of the Lord said to Philip, "Go south to the road—the desert road—that goes down from Jerusalem to Gaza." So he started out, and on his way he met an Ethiopian eunuch, an important official in charge of all the treasury of Candace, queen of the Ethiopians. This man had gone to Jerusalem to worship, and on his way home was sitting in his chariot reading the book of Isaiah the prophet. The Spirit told Philip, "Go to that chariot and stay near it."

Then Philip ran up to the chariot and heard the man reading Isaiah the prophet. "Do you understand what you are reading?" Philip asked.

Then Philip began with that very passage of Scripture and told him the good news about Jesus.

Acts 8:4–8, 26–30, 35

When You Think about It

The story begins in the midst of an exciting revival. Bold Christians were proclaiming Christ from village to village. The Spirit of God was working. The atmosphere was electric. If you've ever been a part of a scene like this, you need no further explanation. If you haven't, you cannot imagine the excitement.

Suddenly, God steps in and does something strange. Without prior announcement—out of the clear blue—He dispatches an angel from heaven and redirects a man named Philip.

How easy it would have been for Philip to be caught up in the excitement and electricity of that Samaritan revival—where God was obviously at work—that he wasn't sensitive to a new direction. Not this man! He was alert and ready. Each day marked a new beginning. He had walked with God long enough to know that He has the right to throw a surprise curve—*and often does!*

Without stating His reason, without revealing the ultimate plan, God led Philip away from Samaria and out onto a desert road. The man was so sensitive to God's leading, there was no struggle.
—Charles Swindoll

Two words in the Christian's language cannot go together: No, Lord.
—Henry Blackaby

> **CHARACTER CHECK**
>
> The biggest hindrance to spiritual deafness (besides willful sin, of course) is the racetrack pace of life. Do what you have to do to go slow enough to hear God when He speaks.

Simon THE SORCERER
Wanting God Selfishly

from Acts 8

Simon was tuned in to the spirit world. Y'know, you don't have to be a Christian to have a flair for the mystical. So naturally, he was intrigued by this Jesus worship. And especially the magic tricks His followers did. He would soon find out it wasn't magic. It was serious.

First, a Quick Read

Now for some time a man named Simon had practiced sorcery in the city and amazed all the people of Samaria. He boasted that he was someone great, and all the people, both high and low, gave him their attention and exclaimed, "This man is the divine power known as the Great Power." They followed him because he had amazed them for a long time with his magic. . . .

When Simon saw that the Spirit was given at the laying on of the apostles' hands, he offered them money and said, "Give me also this ability so that everyone on whom I lay my hands may receive the Holy Spirit."

Peter answered: "May your money perish with you, because you thought you could buy the gift of God with money! You have no part or share in this ministry, because your heart is not right before God. Repent of this wickedness and pray to the Lord. Perhaps he will forgive you for having such a thought in your heart. For I see that you are full of bitterness and captive to sin."

Then Simon answered, "Pray to the Lord for me so that nothing you have said may happen to me."

Acts 8:9–11, 18–24

LOOK AT IT THIS WAY

When will we realize that the goosebumps are a bonus? They're not the main feature. When will we realize that our spiritual triumphs are not given to impress our spiritual friends? They're to encourage the believer and attract attention (to God) from those He is seeking.

The pull of pride and selfishness probably will never let up on us. But as we truly devote ourselves to God, as we genuinely seek His will, as we honestly confess that we want Him to get the glory, He'll give us the strength to push the pull down.

When You Think about It

In the '90s there is a trend toward increasing one's self-esteem. Consequently, we seem to be searching for a God who will help us feel OK about ourselves.

All this reminds me of "The Temple of the Thousand Buddhas," an unusual place of worship in Kyoto, Japan, where worshipers can literally design their own deity. The temple is filled with more than a thousand likenesses of Buddha—each one a little different from the next. Worshipers can pick and choose which they like best. Devotees of Buddha often try to find the likeness they feel most resembles themselves. Then they bow before it in worship. Isn't this a bit like many churchgoers in the '90s?

At the expense of reverence for His sovereignty, we have made God over into a comfortable pal, a "user-friendly" God who makes allowances for our sin and excuses for our backgrounds. There is a word to describe modifying God's laws in this manner—*idolatry*. The great Bible teacher Martyn Lloyd-Jones once wrote that people who teach that God is love without teaching that He hates sin are presenting another god—essentially Satan with a mask on.

—Greg Laurie

There is a place in the religious experience where we love God for Himself alone, with never a thought of His benefits.

—A. W. Tozer

> **CHARACTER CHECK**
>
> We all possess a tendency to want God for what He can do for us. But remember today that if you'll let God use you for what *He* wants, He'll make sure you get taken care of.

Ananias
Believing in Forgiveness
from Acts 9

Ananias had good reason to be a little scared. Saul of Tarsus wasn't just your average convert—IF HE REALLY WAS CONVERTED—and with just the slightest wobble in his own spiritual perception, Ananias could be heading for a date with the dungeon. Watch him work.

First, a Quick Read

In Damascus there was a disciple named Ananias. The Lord called to him in a vision, "Ananias!"

"Yes, Lord," he answered.

The Lord told him, "Go to the house of Judas on Straight Street and ask for a man from Tarsus named Saul, for he is praying. In a vision he has seen a man named Ananias come and place his hands on him to restore his sight."

"Lord," Ananias answered, "I have heard many reports about this man and all the harm he has done to your saints in Jerusalem. And he has come here with authority from the chief priests to arrest all who call on your name."

But the Lord said to Ananias, "Go! This man is my chosen instrument to carry my name before the Gentiles and their kings and before the people of Israel. I will show him how much he must suffer for my name."

Then Ananias went to the house and entered it. Placing his hands on Saul, he said, "Brother Saul, the Lord—Jesus, who appeared to you on the road as you were coming here—has sent me so that you may see again and be filled with the Holy Spirit."

Acts 9:10–17

LOOK AT IT THIS WAY

You've seen him walk into church. The man whose wife and children have been coming by themselves for years. The man who reportedly told the preacher not to ever bother coming to visit him again—ever! He wants to become a Christian. People go down to shake his hand, but their smiles have that I'll-believe-it-when-I-see-it look, that see-if-he's-still-here-this-time-next-year look. He's not asking to be a deacon. He just wants to give his life to Christ. Doesn't God do that here anymore?

When You Think about It

Let me think of the worst individual I know, the one for whom I have no affinity, the one who is a continual thorn in my flesh, who is as mean as can be; can I imagine that person being presented perfect in Christ Jesus? It ought to be an easy thing for the Christian who thinks, to conceive of any and every kind of person being presented perfect in Christ Jesus, but how seldom do we think! If I am an earnest evangelical preacher, I may say to someone, "Oh, yes, I believe God can save you," while in my heart of hearts I don't believe there is much hope for him. Our unbelief stands as the supreme barrier to Jesus Christ's work in people's souls. But once let me get over my slowness of heart to believe in Jesus Christ's power to save, and I become a real generator of His power to others. Are we banking in unshaken faith on the redemption, or do we allow men's sins and wrongs to so obliterate Jesus Christ's power to save that we hinder His reaching them?
—Oswald Chambers

How can you dismiss a soul until God's work is complete?
—Max Lucado

CHARACTER CHECK

Ask God to give you a new heart for the lost—a heart that breaks over men and women who are rejecting His love and kindness, a heart that believes when God gets through.

Barnabas
Encouraging Others
from Acts 11

Barnabas is a smile and a pat on the back. A laugh that starts at his eyes and doesn't stop till the whole room's looking to see what's so funny. But he's the kind of friend who's not just telling you what you want to hear. You can tell he really means it. That's Barnabas.

First, a Quick Read

Now those who had been scattered by the persecution in connection with Stephen traveled as far as Phoenicia, Cyprus and Antioch, telling the message only to Jews. Some of them, however, men from Cyprus and Cyrene, went to Antioch and began to speak to Greeks also, telling them the good news about the Lord Jesus. The Lord's hand was with them, and a great number of people believed and turned to the Lord.

News of this reached the ears of the church at Jerusalem, and they sent Barnabas to Antioch. When he arrived and saw the evidence of the grace of God, he was glad and encouraged them all to remain true to the Lord with all their hearts. He was a good man, full of the Holy Spirit and faith, and a great number of people were brought to the Lord.

Then Barnabas went to Tarsus to look for Saul, and when he found him, he brought him to Antioch. So for a whole year Barnabas and Saul met with the church and taught great numbers of people. The disciples were called Christians first at Antioch.

Acts 11:19–26

LOOK AT IT THIS WAY

Encouragement takes time because encouragement is much more than words. Encouragement is a lifestyle. It's a deliberate, watchful way of giving people the value God says they deserve and blessing them with investments from the wealth of your thoughtfulness.

It works at church, at the office, at the health club, at Little League practice—and it works best at home, where your spouse and children will feast on your kindnesses and genuine compliments. Encouragement is a gift you can start sharing today. Surely you know someone who's starved for a little.

When You Think about It

The Body is growing, and the Word is spreading like a flame. It's too big for the leaders to handle. Assistance is needed: gifted assistance. What does Barnabas do? He searches for and finds Saul of Tarsus, who was an outcast because of his former life. Not afraid to stick his neck out for a new Christian who was suspect in the eyes of the public, Barnabas took him by the hand and brought him to Antioch. Before the entire assembly, the "Son of Encouragement" gave his new friend a push into a priority position—in fact, it was into the very place where Barnabas himself had been experiencing remarkable blessing as a church leader.

Without a thought of jealousy, he later allowed Saul to take the leadership and set the pace for the first missionary journey. It is interesting to note that the names were soon switched from "Barnabas and Saul" to "Paul and Barnabas." It takes a great person to recognize that a man younger than he is has God-given abilities, and to encourage him to move ahead with full support.

Oh, the need for this ministry. Encouragement! Pass it around.
—Charles Swindoll

Correction does much, but encouragement does more.
—Johann Von Goethe

CHARACTER CHECK

If you want to make sure your encouragement doesn't come off sounding phony, just make sure it's not. Ask God to show you how to truly be glad for other's success.

The Philippian Jailer
Accepting the Gospel
from Acts 16

He could tell this was going to be no ordinary night at the lock-up from the very beginning. First, these prisoners won't stop singing, then an earthquake rattles the doors off their hinges. Jailbreak. Pandemonium. And now he's just added a bazillion years to his life. Wow!

First, a Quick Read

About midnight Paul and Silas were praying and singing hymns to God, and the other prisoners were listening to them. Suddenly there was such a violent earthquake that the foundations of the prison were shaken. At once all the prison doors flew open, and everybody's chains came loose. The jailer woke up, and when he saw the prison doors open, he drew his sword and was about to kill himself because he thought the prisoners had escaped. But Paul shouted, "Don't harm yourself! We are all here!"

The jailer called for lights, rushed in and fell trembling before Paul and Silas. He then brought them out and asked, "Sirs, what must I do to be saved?"

They replied, "Believe in the Lord Jesus, and you will be saved—you and your household." Then they spoke the word of the Lord to him and to all the others in his house. At that hour of the night the jailer took them and washed their wounds; then immediately he and all his family were baptized. The jailer brought them into his house and set a meal before them; he was filled with joy because he had come to believe in God—he and his whole family.

Acts 16:25–34

Look at It This Way

We should never get too business-as-usual with this amazing mystery. Every time someone says yes to God's saving message, the same blood that washed your sins down the drain of redemption flows across time and pours a brand new spirit into that person's life.

Nor should we get so distant from the miracle of conversion that we only see its face from our seat on the church bench. It's the privilege of God's people to share this life-giving story with others and expect God to use our witness to win them over.

When You Think about It

Near the city of Sao José dos Campos, Brazil, is a remarkable facility. Twenty years ago, the Brazilian government turned a prison over to two Christians. The institution was renamed Humaita, and the plan was to run it on Christian principles. With the exception of two full-time staff, all the work is done by inmates. Chuck Colson visited the prison and made this report:

"My guide escorted me to the notorious prison cell once used for torture. Today, he told me, that block houses only a single inmate. Slowly, he swung open the massive door, and I saw the prisoner in that punishment cell: a crucifix, beautifully carved by the Humaita inmates—the prisoner Jesus, hanging on a cross. 'He's doing time for the rest of us,' my guide said softly."

Christ has taken your place. There is no need for you to remain in the cell. Ever hear of a discharged prisoner who wanted to stay? Nor have I. When the doors open, the prisoners leave. The thought of a person preferring jail over freedom doesn't compute. Once the penalty is paid, why live under bondage?

—Max Lucado

The Gospel is to me simply irresistible, and I cannot understand why it is not equally irresistible to every mortal man.

—Blaise Pascal

> **CHARACTER CHECK**
>
> Could it be that you're not so sure you've truly asked Christ into your heart? He's a whisper away, and you're in as good a place as any to ask Him in. See you 'round the throne.

Apollos and Aquila
Teachers of the Word

from Acts 18

The Hellenistic world had no shortage of teachers and philosophers who could expound on all the latest modes of thought and experience circulating around the Grecian region. But there was a new brand of teacher in town. And the textbook felt something like a sword.

Look at It This Way

Bible teaching is so critical in the life of the Christian. Even those who have been around the church for years—many who have tried to give the Scriptures their close, regular attention—can still stumble over many doctrines and concepts.

The answer is faithful Bible teaching, delivered by people who don't just exist to fill a Sunday morning hour but whose hearts breathe the Word, whose minds are enlightened to attract wisdom like a sponge, whose lives paint the pages in real-life colors. Is that what you should be doing? We need you.

First, a Quick Read

After this, Paul left Athens and went to Corinth. There he met a Jew named Aquila, a native of Pontus, who had recently come from Italy with his wife Priscilla, because Claudius had ordered all the Jews to leave Rome. Paul went to see them, and because he was a tentmaker as they were, he stayed and worked with them. . . .

Meanwhile a Jew named Apollos, a native of Alexandria, came to Ephesus. He was a learned man, with a thorough knowledge of the Scriptures. He had been instructed in the way of the Lord, and he spoke with great fervor and taught about Jesus accurately, though he knew only the baptism of John. He began to speak boldly in the synagogue. When Priscilla and Aquila heard him, they invited him to their home and explained to him the way of God more adequately.

When Apollos wanted to go to Achaia, the brothers encouraged him and wrote to the disciples there to welcome him. On arriving, he was a great help to those who by grace had believed. For he vigorously refuted the Jews in public debate, proving from the Scriptures that Jesus was the Christ.

Acts 18:1–3, 24–28

When You Think about It

In order to be true to the Great Commission and to produce a mature church that would reproduce itself, the apostles knew they could not get sidetracked from their primary calling—*to pray* and *to teach the Word of God.*

Of all the activities that were taking place in the church in Jerusalem, it is not accidental that these believers were, first of all, continuing "steadfastly in the apostles' doctrine" or "teaching." It was the "apostles' doctrine that gave direction to everything else that happened in the church in Jerusalem. Christian experience, both at the horizontal, human level (such as fellowship and sharing with each other) and at the vertical, divine level (such as prayer and praise) must have divine guidelines. Without these guidelines, Christians can get sidetracked onto peripheral issues and even depart from the will of God. For example, a "Christ-centered community of love" can quickly digress into a "self-centered community." Therefore, all Christian experience must be rooted in and evaluated by Scripture. In this sense, continuing in the "apostles' doctrine" is foundational to all that we do in the church—and in life.

—Gene Getz

One who receives this Word, and by it salvation, receives along with it the duty of passing this Word on.

—Emil Brunner

> **CHARACTER CHECK**
>
> If God has graced you with the gift of teaching, pour your heart and soul into it. Soak yourself good in the Word each day. And bring it home to us where our hearts can hear.

Julius
Kindness in an Unbeliever

from Acts 27

Paul's stormy journey across the sea to stand trial in Rome was made a bit more bearable by the kindness and concern of the Roman officer in charge of guarding him. Let's hope something of Paul's boldness and bravery rubbed off on Julius before his eternal ship ran aground.

Look at It This Way

Christians don't hold the total market on kindness and concern. Those qualities are gifts from God, and the unconverted who bear them simply don't realize they possess a spark of divine nature.

But don't think that the he-was-such-a-good-person line will be a comfortable one to be carrying on the day when all men have to stand before the Judge of all the world. Kindness is great. It keeps the world from being as bad as it would be without God's grace. But it's a long way from enough to matter for long.

First, a Quick Read

When it was decided that we would sail for Italy, Paul and some other prisoners were handed over to a centurion named Julius, who belonged to the Imperial Regiment. . . .

The next day we landed at Sidon; and Julius, in kindness to Paul, allowed him to go to his friends so they might provide for his needs. From there we put out to sea again and passed to the lee of Cyprus because the winds were against us. . . .

When daylight came, they did not recognize the land, but they saw a bay with a sandy beach, where they decided to run the ship aground if they could.

But the ship struck a sandbar and ran aground. The bow stuck fast and would not move, and the stern was broken to pieces by the pounding of the surf.

The soldiers planned to kill the prisoners to prevent any of them from swimming away and escaping. But the centurion wanted to spare Paul's life and kept them from carrying out their plan. He ordered those who could swim to jump overboard first and get to land. The rest were to get there on planks or on pieces of the ship. In this way everyone reached land in safety.

Acts 27:1, 3–4, 39, 41–44

When You Think about It

"Niceness"—wholesome, integrated personality—is an excellent thing. We must try by every medical, educational, economic, and political means in our power, to produce a world where as many people as possible grow up "nice"; just as we must try to produce a world where all have plenty to eat. But we must not suppose that even if we succeeded in making everyone nice, we should have saved their souls. A world of nice people, content in their own niceness, looking no further, turned away from God, would be just as desperately in need of salvation as a miserable world—and might even be more difficult to save.

For mere improvement is no redemption, though redemption always improves people even here and now, and will, in the end, improve them to a degree we cannot yet imagine. God became man to turn creatures into sons: not simply to produce better men of the old kind, but to produce a new kind of man. It is not like teaching a horse to jump better and better, but like turning a horse into a winged creature.

—C. S. Lewis

If they are not righteous even as he is righteous, they are not saved, whatever be their gladness or their content; they are but on the way to be saved.

—George MacDonald

> **CHARACTER CHECK**
>
> Thank God for the kindness of even the non-Christian people around us. But let's be careful not to let their compassion cloud their need for Jesus Christ.

Onesimus
From Useless to Useful
from Philemon

Onesimus had been the servant of one of Paul's pals, Philemon, but had robbed his master and headed for the border. Somewhere along the escape route, however, Jesus Christ had overtaken him and put him in contact with Paul, who writes back to Philemon to say—

LOOK AT IT THIS WAY

Perhaps the greatest miracle of all is that the God who created all there is, who is ultimate perfection, who could choose anything to do His work with (or simply do it Himself—if you want something done right, you know)—chooses to use us.

US! If He has that much confidence in what He can do through us, we are crazy to think that we can't do it, that we aren't any good, that we never will amount to anything. God has hand-picked us for His service. What are we waiting for?

First, a Quick Read

I then, as Paul—an old man and now also a prisoner of Christ Jesus—I appeal to you for my son Onesimus, who became my son while I was in chains. Formerly he was useless to you, but now he has become useful both to you and to me.

I am sending him—who is my very heart—back to you. I would have liked to keep him with me so that he could take your place in helping me while I am in chains for the gospel. But I did not want to do anything without your consent, so that any favor you do will be spontaneous and not forced. Perhaps the reason he was separated from you for a little while was that you might have him back for good—no longer as a slave, but better than a slave, as a dear brother. He is very dear to me but even dearer to you, both as a man and as a brother in the Lord.

So if you consider me a partner, welcome him as you would welcome me. If he has done you any wrong or owes you anything, charge it to me. . . .

Confident of your obedience, I write to you, knowing that you will do even more than I ask.

Philemon 9b–18, 21

When You Think about It

During the first ten years, I worried that my walk with the Lord wasn't good enough. Because I couldn't forget my past sins, I felt very guilty when I thought of all the grace He had shown me. During this time, I used to fall often and then get up again. It seemed that everything—even God—was against me, and that only faith was on my side. Sometimes it got so bad that I thought I was on my way to hell—willfully offending God—and that there was no salvation for me.

Thankfully, these worries did not weaken my faith in God, but actually made it stronger. When I finally reached the point where I expected the rest of my life to be very difficult, I suddenly found myself wholly changed. My soul, which had always been troubled, finally came to rest in a profound inner peace.

I consider God as my King, against whom I've committed all sorts of crimes. Confessing my sins to Him and asking Him to forgive me, I place myself in His hands to do whatever He pleases with me.

—Brother Lawrence

The greatest of all miracles is that we need not be tomorrow what we are today.

—Samuel M. Silver

> **CHARACTER CHECK**
>
> You've been transformed from someone limited by your own potential to someone who is unlimited by God's potential. Trust Him to accomplish whatever He wants to in you.

Paul Struggling with Sin

from Romans 7 & 8

Paul was amazing. How many times have you heard it, or said it yourself—"I wish I could be just like Paul—his courage, his total devotion to Jesus Christ." But even Paul sometimes found himself in the vicious cycle of sin, slugging it out against his own flesh.

Look at It This Way

This is the place where we so often find ourselves—in the frustrating knot of sin and victory, failure and faithfulness, defeat and daring. We could kick ourselves for staying so susceptible to the tired, yet tricky lines of the devil and our own propensity to sin.

But like Paul so powerfully declares: "Thanks be to God." There's a way out of this mess, and His name is Jesus Christ. And if we'll just take Him at His word, we can find ourselves off this runaway roller coaster more often than we're on it.

First, a Quick Read

I know that nothing good lives in me, that is, in my sinful nature. For I have the desire to do what is good, but I cannot carry it out. For what I do is not the good I want to do; no, the evil I do not want to do—this I keep on doing. Now if I do what I do not want to do, it is no longer I who do it, but it is sin living in me that does it.

So I find this law at work: When I want to do good, evil is right there with me. For in my inner being I delight in God's law; but I see another law at work in the members of my body, waging war against the law of my mind and making me a prisoner of the law of sin at work within my members. What a wretched man I am! Who will rescue me from this body of death? Thanks be to God—through Jesus Christ our Lord!

Therefore, there is now no condemnation for those who are in Christ Jesus, because through Christ Jesus the law of the Spirit of life set me free from the law of sin and death.

Romans 7:18–25a; 8:1–2

When You Think about It

An old story is told of a dog sledder in Alaska who owned two dogs: one black and the other white. Once a month he would bring the dogs to town and pit them against one another, taking bets from the townspeople on which dog would win. Sometimes the white dog would be victorious; on other occasions the black dog would win. The fights were not fixed; in fact, they were quite ferocious—but the owner always bet on the winning dog. When he finally stopped fighting the animals, he was asked how he could always tell which dog would win. "That's easy," he replied. "The one I feed."

How do we win? How does the new nature conquer the old nature? How does the spirit overcome the flesh? We win in the battle of the mind. What are we feeding our mind? What are we watching? What are we reading? What are we listening to? What are we thinking of? What does the landscape of our private world look like? We must be hungry for God—and for the goodness that a life with Him yields.

—Ed Young

Our old man is crucified, but he is long a-dying.
—Charles Spurgeon

> **CHARACTER CHECK**
>
> Yes, thanks be to God. By reckoning ourselves as dead to sin—the position we've been given by being crucified with Christ on the cross—we can lose our feeling for temptation.

Paul
Love for His People

from Romans 9; 10; 11

The Jews weren't too crazy about Paul. After all, he had turned on them—gone over to the other side. But if those who opposed him would just listen to him, if they could just see that his ministry was designed to bring blessing to the Jewish people. Please?

LOOK AT IT THIS WAY

Israel has a pivotal role in history. And Romans 9–11 paints a pretty clear picture. God originated His covenant with Israel—picked them right out as His chosen people. But they rejected Him—never more cruelly than when they crucified His only Son. As a result, God chose a people who "once . . . were not a people" (1 Pet. 2:10)—the Gentiles—grafting them into the original promises, with the expressed plan of making the Jews jealous enough for fellowship with God to one day return into the fold. And one day they will.

First, a Quick Read

I speak the truth in Christ—I am not lying, my conscience confirms it in the Holy Spirit—I have great sorrow and unceasing anguish in my heart. For I could wish that I myself were cursed and cut off from Christ for the sake of my brothers, those of my own race, the people of Israel. . . .

Brothers, my heart's desire and prayer to God for the Israelites is that they may be saved. For I can testify about them that they are zealous for God, but their zeal is not based on knowledge. . . .

I ask then: Did God reject his people? By no means! I am an Israelite myself, a descendant of Abraham, from the tribe of Benjamin. God did not reject his people, whom he foreknew. . . .

Inasmuch as I am the apostle to the Gentiles, I make much of my ministry in the hope that I may somehow arouse my own people to envy and save some of them. For if their rejection is the reconciliation of the world, what will their acceptance be but life from the dead?

Romans 9:1–4a; 10:1–2; 11:1–2a, 13b–15

When You Think about It

Paul would be willing to undergo the greatest misery to do the Jews good. He would be content to be cut off from the land of the living, in the most shameful and ignominious manner. He would be content to be excommunicated from the society of the faithful, to be separated from the church, and from the communion of saints, as a heathen man and a publican, if that would do them good. He could wish himself no more remembered among the saints, his name blotted out of the church records; though he had been so great a planter of churches, and the spiritual father of so many thousands, yet he would be content to be disowned by the church, cut off from the communion of it, and have his name buried in oblivion or reproach, for the good of the Jews.

We ought to be in a special manner concerned for the spiritual good of our relations, our brethren, and kinsmen. To them we lie under special engagements, and we have more opportunity of doing good to them, and our usefulness to them we must in a special manner give account.
—Matthew Henry

Love is the only badge by which the disciples of our Lord Jesus Christ are known.
—D. L. Moody

> **CHARACTER CHECK**
>
> Paul loved his people, had great respect for his heritage. And as you study, watch, and get to know the Jewish people, you'll love them too. They are our forefathers in the faith.

Paul
Love for the Church
from 1 Thessalonians 2 & 3

Paul poured his life into the church. His relationship with the ones he started and sustained was like a father for his children—or, as he said, like a mother—"for whom I am again in the pains of childbirth until Christ is formed in you." There's a lot of love in this passage.

Look at It This Way

The thought of a serious believer existing outside the blessings and boundaries of the local church is a lie in the language of Christian living. God's people are grown to live in relationship, feeding off their Gospel fellowship, partaking of the sacred reminders of the Christian mystery, lifting each other up in believing prayer, and holding each other accountable as flesh-and-blood witnesses for Christ. Love your church. Serve your church. Minister to the needy. Invest yourself in its mission, and find your role in helping bring it to pass.

First, a Quick Read

We loved you so much that we were delighted to share with you not only the gospel of God but our lives as well, because you had become so dear to us. Surely you remember, brothers, our toil and hardship; we worked night and day in order not to be a burden to anyone while we preached the gospel of God to you. . . .

For you know that we dealt with each of you as a father deals with his own children, encouraging, comforting and urging you to live lives worthy of God, who calls you into his kingdom and glory. . . .

For what is our hope, our joy, or the crown in which we will glory in the presence of our Lord Jesus when he comes? Is it not you? Indeed, you are our glory and joy. . . .

Therefore, brothers, in all our distress and persecution we were encouraged about you because of your faith. For now we really live, since you are standing firm in the Lord. How can we thank God enough for you in return for all the joy we have in the presence of our God because of you? Night and day we pray most earnestly that we may see you again and supply what is lacking in your faith.

1 Thessalonians 2:8–10, 11–12, 19–20; 3:7–10

When You Think about It

Church means the body of believers, not the buildings where the believers assemble. It is the group with whom we marry our children, bury our dead, receive comfort in crisis, accept meals in sickness, partake of the Lord's Supper, learn about the character of God, become trained in doctrine, commune with Christ, fellowship with other believers, become discipled in the way we should walk, develop a personal ministry, honor God with our tithes and offerings, bring unsaved friends, hear the preaching of God's Word, express our spiritual gifts, raise our children in spiritual instruction, and take vows for which we are accountable.

Have you ever really considered the depth of the role your church plays in your life and the life of your family? Read that last paragraph again, slowly this time, pausing to give thanks to God for your church.

A great need today is that Christians revalue the church—that they recognize the importance of membership in a vital body of believers. Supporting a local church through membership—not merely attendance—represents the most significant of the public spiritual disciplines. If we truly love Christ, we will want to be around His people.

—Patrick Morley

Imperfect as it is, the church is still the dearest place on earth to us.

—Charles Spurgeon

> **CHARACTER CHECK**
>
> If you're not actively involved in a local Christian church, it's time you followed God's call to the one where He wants you. Take it from those who are already there. You'll love it.

Paul
No Lone Ranger
from Titus 1; 2; 3

As capable and in-charge as Paul was, he never succumbed to the debilitating mistake of taking too much on himself. His habit of sharing the responsibilities of ministry with a trusted team of leaders shows up in nearly all his books. Like in this one, to Titus.

LOOK AT IT THIS WAY

Beyond our hunger for having fellowship with those inside our local churches, we need to draw our lines big enough to take in all those who embrace the Christian faith. If we keep ourselves too sequestered from other expressions of worship and other methods of fulfilling our shared priorities, we'll find ourselves plowing the same ground, wasting many of our efforts, and—worse—growing a little bit competitive with those we're supposed to be on same side with. We're all in this thing together.

First, a Quick Read

To Titus, my true son in our common faith. . . .

The reason I left you in Crete was that you might straighten out what was left unfinished and appoint elders in every town, as I directed you. . . .

Teach the older men to be temperate, worthy of respect, self-controlled, and sound in faith, in love and in endurance.

Likewise, teach the older women to be reverent in the way they live, not to be slanderers or addicted to much wine, but to teach what is good. Then they can train the younger women to love their husbands and children, to be self-controlled and pure, to be busy at home, to be kind, and to be subject to their husbands, so that no one will malign the word of God. Similarly, encourage the young men to be self-controlled. . . .

As soon as I send Artemas or Tychicus to you, do your best to come to me at Nicopolis, because I have decided to winter there. Do everything you can to help Zenas the lawyer and Apollos on their way and see that they have everything they need. . . .

Everyone with me sends you greetings. Greet those who love us in the faith.

Grace be with you all.

Titus 1:4a, 5; 2:2–6; 3:12–13, 15

When You Think about It

Many men have a "Lone Ranger mentality." They live with the belief that they can right the wrongs, beat the world into submission, be successful at everything—and never need anyone's help along the way. The mask they wear is the mask of *denial*. The silver bullets they roll in their fingers are engraved with the word *egotist*.

When Jesus sent the disciples out on their first short missionary journey, He sent them two by two. It wasn't to get better hotel rates or to have argumentative advantage in the sharing of their faith. It was for mutual support and encouragement when things were not going well. He did not want them to be alone in the calling to follow Him.

When the apostle Paul traveled on his missionary journeys planting churches, he brought others along for support, help, and encouragement. Both Paul and Jesus demonstrated the call of the gospel as the call to friendship, like-mindedness, and a supportive community.

God has created us to hunger for relationships. When you deny that hunger, you endanger your own emotional and spiritual well-being.

—Jim Smoke

We have to ride together if we're going to stay in the saddle.

—Stu Weber

> **CHARACTER CHECK**
>
> Look for ways to bridge the denominational and racial barriers that still keep Sunday the most segregated day of the week. Find your unique role in the body of Christ.

Paul
Embracing Hardship
from 2 Corinthians 4 & 11

Unbelievable. What this one man endured for the cause of Christ is beyond most of our imaginations. Lashes, rods, beatings, hunger. Imprisonment, courtrooms, shipwreck, threats. One thing's for sure as we read his letters. This guy believed what he professed.

Look at It This Way

Paul was on a mission, a crusade for Christ. There's something about throwing your whole self into a mighty cause that almost feeds off adversity.

But more often then not, our hardships don't come with such clear reasons or instructions. Yet we know that whatever we face has a benefit buried just below the surface. Or it can be transformed into having one by the God who never allows us to endure more than we can stand. Embrace your hardship as something you can grow from. And let God perform His perfect work.

First, a Quick Read

Five times I received from the Jews the forty lashes minus one. Three times I was beaten with rods, once I was stoned, three times I was shipwrecked, I spent a night and a day in the open sea, I have been constantly on the move. I have been in danger from rivers, in danger from bandits, in danger from my own countrymen, in danger from Gentiles; in danger in the city, in danger in the country, in danger at sea; and in danger from false brothers. I have labored and toiled and have often gone without sleep; I have known hunger and thirst and have often gone without food; I have been cold and naked. . . .

All this is for your benefit, so that the grace that is reaching more and more people may cause thanksgiving to overflow to the glory of God.

Therefore we do not lose heart. Though outwardly we are wasting away, yet inwardly we are being renewed day by day. For our light and momentary troubles are achieving for us an eternal glory that far outweighs them all. So we fix our eyes not on what is seen, but on what is unseen. For what is seen is temporary, but what is unseen is eternal.

2 Corinthians 11:24–27; 4:15–18

When You Think about It

Acceptance of a share, still more the willing acceptance of more than our full share, in the tragedy of life is positive; it has about it something vitalizing. Those who meet pain clear-eyed, and with a positive and active acceptance, who "face the music" as the slang phrase has it; those who are not only ready to do their bit, but to share their bit in the world's sorrow, make a great discovery. They find not only that they are enabled to bear their sorrow in a way which hurts less (for that which hurts most in the bearing is that which is most resented; what is most freely accepted hurts least)—but that they achieve an enrichment and a growth in personality which makes them centers of influence and light, in ways of which they never suspected the possibility. Few things can so inspire and re-create the human heart as the spectacle of crushing misfortune cheerfully and heroically borne; and the unconscious influence which those exert is far greater than they or others comprehend. Suffering lightly borne is constructive work, for pain conquered is power.
—Lily Dougall

We aren't defined by what we are going through, but by how we are going through it.
—Wellington Boone

> **CHARACTER CHECK**
>
> The hardest suffering to endure is the suffering that seems to make no sense. But trust that God has made sense of it and will see you through to a better end.

Paul
Humble before God

from Philippians 3; 1 Corinthians 15; 1 Timothy 1

Paul's natural demeanor was one of cold, calculating efficiency. Today, we'd call him driven. But God had thrown a huge bucket of grace onto the hot coals of his tough-minded temper, and now his hard-driving focus was getting to share space with a calm, gracious humility.

Look at It This Way

Humility before God is a long way from weak-in-the-knees bowing and scraping. There'll come a time for that—for those who choose to wait until humility is forced upon them. But being humble now means accepting his picture of you as the real one—your sins covered by Christ's forgiveness, your heart filled with His Spirit, your will emboldened by the power of Christ's resurrected glory. It's imagining, as Max Lucado says, that if God carried a wallet, he'd have your picture in it. How do you say thank-you for that?

First, a Quick Read

But whatever was to my profit I now consider loss for the sake of Christ. What is more, I consider everything a loss compared to the surpassing greatness of knowing Christ Jesus my Lord, for whose sake I have lost all things. I consider them rubbish, that I may gain Christ.
Philippians 3:7–8

For I am the least of the apostles and do not even deserve to be called an apostle, because I persecuted the church of God.
1 Corinthians 15:9

I thank Christ Jesus our Lord, who has given me strength, that he considered me faithful, appointing me to his service. Even though I was once a blasphemer and a persecutor and a violent man, I was shown mercy because I acted in ignorance and unbelief. The grace of our Lord was poured out on me abundantly, along with the faith and love that are in Christ Jesus. . . .

Christ Jesus came into the world to save sinners—of whom I am the worst. But for that very reason I was shown mercy so that in me, the worst of sinners, Christ Jesus might display his unlimited patience as an example for those who would believe on him and receive eternal life.

1 Timothy 1:12–14, 15b–16

When You Think about It

There are those who exhibit a Pharisaic holiness; they thank God with an arrogant offensiveness that they are not as other men are; they have forgotten the horrible pit and miry clay from where they were taken.

A holy man is not one who has his eyes set on his own whiteness but one who is personally and passionately devoted to the Lord who saved Him—one whom the Holy Spirit takes care shall never forget that God has made him what he is by sheer sovereign grace.

The humility Paul manifests was produced in him by the remembrance that Jesus, whom he had scorned and despised, whose followers he had persecuted, whose church he had harried, had not only forgiven him, but had made him His chief apostle. Show such a servant of God the backslider, the sinner steeped in the iniquity of our cities, and there will spring up in his heart an amazing well of compassion and love for that one, because he himself has experienced the grace of God that goes to the uttermost depths of sin and lifts to the highest heights of salvation.
—Oswald Chambers

Nothing sets a person so much out of the devil's reach as humility.
—Jonathan Edwards

> **CHARACTER CHECK**
>
> Take some time today to reflect again on the beauty of your salvation—remembering the price, recapturing the reality, restoring the joy. It's a great day to be humble.

Paul
Recognizing His Need for Prayer

from Selected Readings

Paul understood that his success in ministry had a direct correlation with the prayers of the saints. He begged for them, pleaded for them, expected something from them—but not so that he could get blessings from God, but that God could share His blessings through him.

Look at It This Way

The prayers of other people on our behalf can become a forgotten piece of our spiritual arsenal. We don't want people to know too much. And even when we do, we doubt that too many of the I'll-be-praying-for-you's ever make it ten feet from the promise—because we know we've failed to keep it for others. Until we believe that prayers are more than a duty, more than comforting thoughts and hollow wish lists, but a mighty force of spiritual dynamite, we'll keep leaking our power. We'll keep ignoring the promise.

First, a Quick Read

Brothers, pray for us.

1 Thessalonians 5:25

Pray also for me, that whenever I open my mouth, words may be given me so that I will fearlessly make known the mystery of the gospel, for which I am an ambassador in chains. Pray that I may declare it fearlessly, as I should.

Ephesians 6:19–20

Finally, brothers, pray for us that the message of the Lord may spread rapidly and be honored, just as it was with you. And pray that we may be delivered from wicked and evil men, for not everyone has faith.

2 Thessalonians 3:1–2

He has delivered us from such a deadly peril, and he will deliver us. On him we have set our hope that he will continue to deliver us, as you help us by your prayers.

2 Corinthians 1:10–11a

And one thing more: Prepare a guest room for me, because I hope to be restored to you in answer to your prayers.

Philemon 22

I, Paul, write this greeting in my own hand. Remember my chains. Grace be with you.

Colossians 4:18

When You Think about It

Satan's desire is to destroy the work of Christ in the world. One of his most effective ways of doing that is to destroy pastors. If Satan can bring them down, causing disgrace and ridicule to taint the work of Christ, the nonbelieving world will not be attracted to Jesus. We have all seen the carnage left around us as pastors have failed morally or have simply left the ministry because of disillusionment.

Pastors need to know their churches are with them and are praying for them, so they can be emboldened to share the whole council of God and not cower in the face of opposition within or without the church.

E. M. Bounds said it this way: "The men in the pew given to praying for the pastor are like poles which hold up the wires along which the electric current runs. They are not the power, neither are they the specific agents in making the Word of the Lord more effective. But they hold up the wires upon which the divine power runs to the hearts of men. They make conditions favorable for the preaching of the Gospel."

—Dale Schlafer

Let me have your prayers, and I can do anything! Let me be without my people's prayers, and I can do nothing.

—Charles Spurgeon

> **CHARACTER CHECK**
>
> You depend on other's prayers much more than you know, just as they depend on yours for their godly power and strength. Find someone you know will keep a promise.

John
Appealing for Love

from 1 John 3 & 2 John

John was known as the apostle Christ loved. And love set the tone for his legacy. He had discovered the secret of Christian living, the unifying bond between different classes of people, and the mark that would distinguish the church in the world. Love. Love never fails.

LOOK AT IT THIS WAY

Love is the most unnatural of the virtues. Perhaps that's why God has earmarked it as the defining characteristic of His people. It must fight every shred of self; it must quiet every shout of discord. It can only be truly fashioned in people who have been made unnatural themselves, who have been transformed into new creatures.

So love is our mark. It will remain after faith has finally seen its object, after hope has finally held its reward. Love will last forever because it's being grown in the people who will live forever.

First, a Quick Read

The elder, To the chosen lady and her children, whom I love in the truth—and not I only, but also all who know the truth—because of the truth, which lives in us and will be with us forever:

Grace, mercy and peace from God the Father and from Jesus Christ, the Father's Son, will be with us in truth and love.

It has given me great joy to find some of your children walking in the truth, just as the Father commanded us.

2 John 1–4

And this is his command: to believe in the name of his Son, Jesus Christ, and to love one another as he commanded us.

1 John 3:23

And now, dear lady, I am not writing you a new command but one we have had from the beginning. I ask that we love one another. And this is love: that we walk in obedience to his commands. As you have heard from the beginning, his command is that you walk in love. . . .

I have much to write to you, but I do not want to use paper and ink. Instead, I hope to visit you and talk with you face to face, so that our joy may be complete.

2 John 5–6, 12

When You Think about It

Though natural likings should normally be encouraged, it would be quite wrong to think that the way to become charitable is to sit trying to manufacture affectionate feelings. Do not waste time bothering whether you "love" your neighbor; act as if you did. As soon as we do this, we find one of the great secrets. When you are behaving as if you loved someone, you will presently come to love him.

If you injure someone you dislike, you will find yourself disliking him more. If you do to him a good turn, not to please God and obey the law of charity, but to show him what a fine forgiving chap you are, and to put him in your debt, and then sit down to wait for his "gratitude," you will probably be disappointed. (People are not fools: they have a very quick eye for anything like showing off, or patronage.) But whenever we do good to another self, just because it is a self, made (like us) by God, and desiring its own happiness as we desire ours, we shall have learned to love it a little more.
—C. S. Lewis

One's love for God is equal to the love one has for the man he loves least.
—John J. Hugo

> **CHARACTER CHECK**
>
> Love draws you about as close to the heart of God as you can get. You'll probably face a situation today that will give you the option of using it—and letting you see for yourself.

John
Open to God's Revelation

from Revelation 1

Stranded on the island of Patmos, about as far away from everything he'd ever known as he could be, John never thought he'd be used by God again. But he continued taking time on the Lord's Day to meet with God in worship. And one day something unbelievable happened.

First, a Quick Read

I, John, your brother and companion in the suffering and kingdom and patient endurance that are ours in Jesus, was on the island of Patmos because of the word of God and the testimony of Jesus. On the Lord's Day I was in the Spirit, and I heard behind me a loud voice like a trumpet, which said: "Write on a scroll what you see and send it to the seven churches: to Ephesus, Smyrna, Pergamum, Thyatira, Sardis, Philadelphia and Laodicea."

I turned around to see the voice that was speaking to me. And when I turned I saw seven golden lampstands, and among the lampstands was someone "like a son of man," dressed in a robe reaching down to his feet and with a golden sash around his chest. . . .

When I saw him, I fell at his feet as though dead. Then he placed his right hand on me and said: "Do not be afraid. I am the First and the Last. I am the Living One; I was dead, and behold I am alive for ever and ever! And I hold the keys of death and Hades.

"Write, therefore, what you have seen, what is now and what will take place later."

Revelation 1:9–13, 17–19

LOOK AT IT THIS WAY

"Even when I am old and gray, / do not forsake me, O God, / till I declare your power to the next generation, / your might to all who are to come" (Ps. 71:18). The cry of the psalmist, longing to be used until his dying breath, seeing the lasting importance of passing down a godly heritage to his children and grandchildren, reveals the kind of heart we all should have. Even when we're old and gray, Lord, use us. Keep us open. Keep us right where you want us to be.

When You Think about It

All of us are faced with two realms of reality. We deal with the visible, the tangible every day. We know that it is real. But there is another world, another realm of reality which vies for our attention. The spiritual, the heavenly, and the eternal! The door which John saw open was the door between earth and heaven, the aperture between the visible reality and the invisible reality.

Amid all that bids you run and hide and flounder in hopelessness, don't you see that same open door? Don't you hear that same thunderous voice bidding you to come and see? Don't you see that throne and he who sits upon it? He is not wringing his hands over a world catapulting into oblivion. He does not walk around the throne with furrowed brow and worried look. He is the Sovereign God. He is running the show! Get your philosophy of history in line with that, and you will be prepared to praise. Repent of the sin of believing that things are as they appear to be. Ask God to reshape your whole perspective around the vision of God on a throne.

—Jack Taylor

God wants to get your mind racing and your heart beating with a present-tense excitement, a right-around-the-corner anticipation of heaven.

—Joni Eareckson Tada

> **CHARACTER CHECK**
>
> Make it your goal in old age to keep your ear tuned more sharply to God's voice, following him faithfully all the way to the end. This is a lifetime deal. No quitters need apply.

Sources

3 Lawrence F. Burtoft, *Reclaiming the Culture* (Focus on the Family), 82–83; Ben Jonson, quoted in *Reclaiming the Culture* (Focus on the Family), 82–83.

5 Oswald Chambers, *My Utmost for His Highest* (Barbour), May 25; John Calvin, quoted in *Intentional Integrity* (B&H), 123.

7 Andrew Murray, *Daily Secrets of Christian Living* (Kregel), January 1; William Law, quoted in *Let Prayer Change Your Life* (Nelson), 170.

9 Gene Getz, *Men of Character: Abraham* (B&H), 179; F. B. Meyer, quoted in *Men of Character: Abraham* (B&H), 176.

11 C. Welton Gaddy, *A Love Affair with God* (B&H), 140–41; G. Campbell Morgan, quoted in *Prayer: Life's Limitless Reach* (B&H), 130.

13 Tom Sirotnak, *Ultimate Warriors* (B&H), 149–51; Dwight D. Eisenhower, quoted in *Ultimate Warriors* (B&H), 128.

15 Chip Ricks, *The Plans of His Heart* (B&H), 167, 170; Francis of Assisi, quoted in *Classic Quotes on Contemporary Issues* (Shaw), 108.

17 Josh McDowell, *The Father Connection* (B&H), 45–46; T. W. Hunt, *The Mind of Christ* (B&H), 11.

19 Henry Blackaby, *Experiencing God* (B&H), 20; Keith Brooks, quoted in *Dad's Appreciation Book of Wisdom* (Shaw), 94.

21 James R. Lucas, *Walking through the Fire* (B&H), 22–24; Viktor Frankl, quoted in *Values and Virtues* (Multnomah), 14.

23 Charles Swindoll, *Man to Man* (Zondervan), 203–4; Truett Cathy, quoted in *All Preachers Great and Small* (Shaw), 27.

25 Charles Spurgeon, *Morning and Evening* (Hendrickson), July 24; quote from *Basic Training* (Nelson), 136.

27 John Maxwell, *The Success Journey* (Nelson), 101; John Wooden, quoted in *The Success Journey* (Nelson), 101.

29 Charles Stanley, *The Wonderful Spirit-Filled Life* (Nelson), 147–48; A. W. Pink, quoted on *Christian Quotation of the Day* (Gospelcom.net), 4–19–97.

31 John Eldredge, *Reclaiming the Culture* (Focus on the Family), 108–9, 115; Abraham Lincoln, quoted in *Reclaiming the Culture* (Focus on the Family), 108.

33 *Matthew Henry: A Commentary on the Whole Bible* (Revell), Vol. 1; Forbes W. Robertson, quoted in *Christian Quotation of the Day* (Gospelcom.net), 2–1–97.

35 L. H. Hardwick, Jr., Christ Church sermon (with permission), 6–22–97; William J. Bennett, quoted in *Along the Road to Manhood* (Multnomah), 29.

37 Greg Laurie, *The Great Compromise* (Word), 194–96; Jim Elliot, quoted in *A Touch of His Love* (Nelson), 115.

39 Joe Wright, quoted in *Basic Training* (Nelson); Chuck Colson, quoted in *Jubilee* (publisher unknown), July/August 1993.

41 Gene Getz, *Men of Character: Joshua* (B&H), 57–58; John Owen, quoted on *Christian Quotation of the Day* (Gospelcom.net), 7–20–96.

43 C. W. Brister, *Dealing with Doubt* (B&H), 13, 18–20; John Maxwell, quoted on *Living at the Next Level* (Nelson), 91.

45 Dietrich Gruen, *Fathers Who Made a Difference* (Bethany House), 38; *3,000 Quotations from George MacDonald* (Revell), 345.

47 O. S. Hawkins, *Moral Earthquakes* (B&H), 27; *The Confessions of St. Augustine* (Whitaker House), 96.

49 William Law, *A Practical Treatise upon Christian Perfection*; Lloyd John Ogilvie, quoted in *Silent Strength for My Life* (Harvest House).

51 Charles Spurgeon, *A Passion for Holiness in a Believer's Life* (Emerald Books), 189–90; unknown source.
53 Millard MacAdam, *Intentional Integrity* (B&H), 20; Catherine of Siena, quoted in *Classic Quotes on Contemporary Issues* (Shaw), 123.
55 Jim Henry, *Keeping Life in Perspective* (B&H), 137; William Penn, quoted in *Values and Virtues* (Multnomah), 110.
57 Gene Getz, *Men of Character:David* (B&H), 123; Charles Swindoll, *David* (Word), 93.
59 Robert Webber, *Blended Worship* (Hendrickson), 5; William Temple, quoted on *Christian Quotation of the Day* (Gospelcom.net), 9–27–96.
61 Oswald Chambers, *Conformed to His Image* (Discovery House), 77; Mother Teresa, quoted in *God's Treasury of Virtues* (Honor), 232.
63 Charles Spurgeon, *A Passion for Holiness in a Believer's Life* (Emerald Books), 24; William Law, quoted on *Christian Quotation of the Day* (Gospelcom.net), 4–26–96.
65 Charles Swindoll, *David* (Word), 288; George Seaver, quoted on *Christian Quotation of the Day* (Gospelcom.net), 1–19–97.
67 Gary Smalley and John Trent, *The Blessing* (Pocket Books), 89, 92; Bert Ghezzi, quoted in *Along the Road to Manhood* (Multnomah), 53.
69 Donald Whitney, *Spiritual Disciplines for the Christian Life* (Navpress), 141; Martin Luther, quoted on *Christian Quotation of the Day* (Gospelcom.net), 2–15–96.
71 Ray Pritchard, *The ABCs of Wisdom* (Moody), 314–16; *3,000 Quotations from George MacDonald* (Revell), 340.
73 C. S. Lewis, *God in the Dock* (Inspirational Press), 331–33; G. K. Chesterton, quoted in *Been There, Done That, Now What?* (B&H), 11.
75 *Matthew Henry's Commentary on the Whole Bible* (Revell), Vol. 2; Ed Cole, *Strong Men in Tough Times* (Creation House), 45.
77 Jim Gilbert, *How a Man Stands Up for Christ* (Bethany House), 55, 59–60; Lee Strobel, quoted in *D. L. Moody's Little Instruction Book* (Honor), 83.
79 James Baldwin, *The Book of Virtues* (Simon & Schuster), 67–68; A. W. Tozer, *Inside the Mind of Unchurched Harry and Mary* (Zondervan), 83.
81 Gordon MacDonald, *Renewing Your Spiritual Passion* (Inspirational Press), 216–17; George MacDonald, quoted on *Christian Quotation of the Day* (Gospelcom.net), 9–2–96.
83 Tom Sirotnak, *Ultimate Warriors* (B&H), 28–30; John Milton, quoted in *Classic Quotes on Contemporary Issues* (Shaw), 57.
85 Quoted in *America's God and Country* (Fame Publishing), 599–601; quoted in *America's God and Country* (Fame Publishing), 660.
87 Howard Hendrick, *Seven Promises of a Promise Keeper* (Focus on the Family), 53–55; James Dobson, *Parenting Isn't for Cowards* (Word).
89 Dan Scott, *The Emerging of the American Church* (Bristol Books), 326–27, 353; John Burroughs, quoted in *The Christian's Treasury* (Crossway), 36.
91 Steve Farrar, *Finishing Strong* (Multnomah), 102–3, 108; C. S. Lewis, quoted in *Finishing Strong* (Multnomah), 108.
93 Norman Harrison, quoted in *Let Prayer Change Your Life* (Nelson), 103–4; John Calvin, quoted in *Classic Quotes on Contemporary Issues* (Shaw), 50.
95 Henry Blackaby, *Fresh Encounter* (B&H), 208–9; Charles Finney, quoted in *America's God and Country* (Fame Publishing), 235.
97 *Moments of Meditation from Matthew Henry* (Zondervan), July 12; quoted in *Martin Luther's Little Instruction Book* (Honor), 79.
99 Gene Getz, *Men of Character: Nehemiah* (B&H), 139–40; Thomas Carlyle, quoted in *Men of Character: Nehemiah* (B&H), 136.

101 Francis Shaeffer, *Whatever Happened to the Human Race?* (Crossway), 1–2; Ron Sider, quoted in *Light* (Christian Life Commission), July/August 1995.
103 Oswald Chambers, *My Utmost for His Highest* (Barbour), 195, 219; Wellington Boone, *Breaking Through* (B&H), 85.
105 Amy Carmichael, *A Very Present Help* (Servant), 90–91; Samuel Johnson, quoted in *Values and Virtues* (Multnomah), 78.
107 A. W. Tozer, *The Knowledge of the Holy* (Harper), 110–12; Hugh Black, quoted in *3,000 Quotations from George MacDonald* (Revell), 86.
109 Henry Blackaby, *The Power of the Call* (B&H), 142–44; Dag Hammarskjold, quoted in *Living at the Next Level* (Nelson), 89.
111 Jim Henry, *Keeping Life in Perspective* (B&H), 108–9; Richard Niebuhr, *Christ and Culture* (Harper).
113 Evelyn Underhill, quoted in *God's Treasury of Virtues* (Honor), 298; *John Wesley's Little Instruction Book* (Honor), 102.
115 Watchman Nee, *The Normal Christian Life* (Tyndale), 107; *A. W. Tozer's Little Instruction Book* (Honor), 74.
117 *Holman Bible Handbook* (B&H), 498–99; Corrie ten Boom, quoted in *The Great Compromise* (Word), 171.
119 Frederick Buechner, *The Longing for Home* (Harper), 120–22; *1,100 Illustrations from D. L. Moody* (Baker), 98.
121 Henry Blackaby, *Experiencing God* (B&H), 146, 150, 153; George W. Truett, quoted in *The Glorious Journey* (Nelson), 228.
123 Watchman Nee, *The Normal Christian Life* (Tyndale), 264–65; André Gide, quoted in *Living at the Next Level* (Nelson), 84.
125 Gordon MacDonald, *Ordering Your Private World* (Inspirational Press), 56; Chuck Colson, quoted in *Words of Promise* (Creation House), 6.
127 C. S. Lewis, *Mere Christianity* (Macmillan), 63–64; W. Phillip Keller, quoted in *The Get-Well Book* (Shaw), 10.
129 Andrew Murray, *With Christ in the School of Prayer* (Whitaker), 74–75; Blaise Pascal, quoted in *The Christian's Treasury* (Crossway), 92.
131 *1,100 Illustrations of D. L. Moody* (Baker), 67–68; John R. W. Stott, *Basic Christianity* (Eerdmans), 111.
133 C. S. Lewis, *Surprised by Joy* (Inspirational Press), 125; *The Confessions of St. Augustine.*
135 Francis Shaeffer, *Whatever Happened to the Human Race* (Crossway), 127; F. LaGard Smith, *Meeting God in Quiet Places* (Harvest House), 31.
137 Elisabeth Elliot, quoted in *God's Treasury of Virtues* (Honor), 231–32; Brother Lawrence, *The Practice of the Presence of God.*
139 F. LaGard Smith, *Meeting God in Quiet Places* (Harvest House), 119, 121; *2,200 Quotations from Charles Spurgeon* (Baker), 45.
141 Henry Blackaby, *Experiencing God* (B&H), 170, 172; Charles Stanley, quoted in *The Glorious Journey* (Nelson), 267.
143 Ray Pritchard, *The ABCs of Wisdom* (Moody), 242–43; Vance Havner, *Truth for Each Day* (Revell), 150.
145 Wellington Boone, *Breaking Through* (B&H), 94, 98; Phillip Porter, *Let the Walls Fall Down* (Creation House), 15.
147 Chuck Colson, *In the Lion's Den* (B&H), Foreword; *3,000 Quotations from George MacDonald* (Baker), 286.
149 Charles Swindoll, *Strengthening Your Grip* (Word), 227–28; Henry Blackaby, quoted in *Words of Promise* (Creation House), 35.
151 Greg Laurie, *The Great Compromise* (Word), 7–8, 14; *A. W. Tozer's Little Instruction Book* (Honor), 28.

153 Oswald Chambers, *Conformed to His Image* (Discovery House), 12–13; Max Lucado, *In the Grip of Grace* (Word), 40.
155 Charles Swindoll, *Growing Strong in the Seasons of Life* (Multnomah), 142–43; Johann Von Goethe, quoted in *New Every Morning* (Multnomah), March 9.
157 Max Lucado, *In the Grip of Grace* (Word), 112–13; Blaise Pascal, quoted in *Conformed to His Image* (Discovery House), 12.
159 Gene Getz, *The Walk* (B&H)110; Emil Brunner, quoted on *Christian Quotation of the Day* (Gospelcom.net), 5–10–97.
161 C. S. Lewis, *Mere Christianity* (Macmillan), 182; *3,000 Quotations from George MacDonald* (Baker), 286.
163 Brother Lawrence, *The Practice of the Presence of God* (Whitaker), 36–37; Samuel M. Silver, quoted in *Living at the Next Level* (Nelson), 13.
165 Ed Young, *Been There, Done That, Now What?* (B&H), 200–201; Charles Spurgeon, *A Passion for Holiness in a Believer's Life* (Emerald Books), 33.
167 *Matthew Henry's Commentary on the Whole Bible* (Revell), Vol. 6; *1,100 Illustrations of D. L. Moody* (Baker), 179.
169 Patrick Morley, *Seven Seasons of a Man's Life* (Nelson), 216–17; *2,200 Quotations from the Writings of Charles Spurgeon* (Baker), 32.
171 Jim Smoke, *How a Man Measures Success* (Bethany House), 22, 27; Stu Weber, *Locking Arms* (Multnomah), 222.
173 Lily Dougall, quoted in *Salute to a Sufferer* (Abingdon), 88–89; Wellington Boone, *Breaking Through* (B&H), 120.
175 Oswald Chambers, *Conformed to His Image* (Discovery House), 117–19; Jonathan Edwards, quoted in *The Complete Speaker's Sourcebook* (Zondervan), 128.
177 Dale Schafer, *Seven Promises of a Promise Keeper* (Focus on the Family), 137–38; *2,200 Quotations from the Writings of Charles Spurgeon* (Baker), 152.
179 C. S. Lewis, *Mere Christianity* (Macmillan), 116; John J. Hugo, quoted in *The Complete Speaker's Sourcebook* (Zondervan), 155.
181 Jack Taylor, *The Hallelujah Factor* (B&H), 23, 25; Joni Eareckson Tada, *Heaven* (Zondervan), 130.